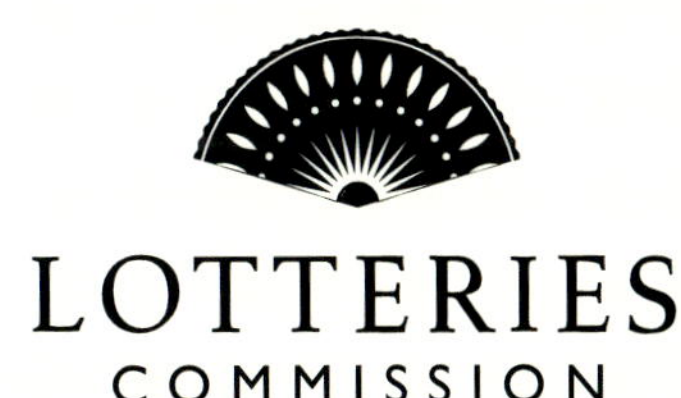

LOTTERIES
COMMISSION

Sponsored by the Lotteries Commission of Western Australia

MICHAEL O'FERRALL

Jimmy Pike

— DESERT DESIGNS

1981–1995

ART GALLERY OF WESTERN AUSTRALIA

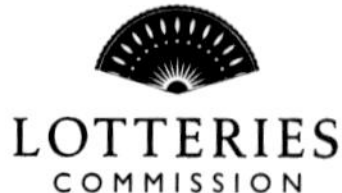

LOTTERIES
COMMISSION

Sponsored by the Lotteries Commission of Western Australia

This catalogue was produced to coincide with the exhibition
Jimmy Pike – Desert Designs 1981–1995
26 October – 8 December 1995

Exhibition Curator: Michael O'Ferrall
Curatorial Assistant: Tjalaminu Mia
Photographer: Greg Woodward
Graphic Designer: Trevor Vincent
Editor: Allan Watson
Printer: Scott Four Colour Print, Perth

Published by the Art Gallery of Western Australia,
Perth Cultural Centre, Perth WA 6000
Copyright: Art Gallery of Western Australia

National Library of Australia
Cataloguing-in-publication

Pike, Jimmy.
Jimmy Pike – Desert Designs 1981–1995.

Bibliography.
ISBN 0 7309 3611 2.

1. Pike, Jimmy – Exhibitions.
2. Art, Australian – Western Australia – Aboriginal artists – Exhibitions.
I. O'Ferrall, Michael A. (Michael Anthony), 1945 – .
II. Art Gallery of Western Australia.
III. Title.

759.9940749411

The work reproduced on page 60 has undergone extensive conservation.
However water damage staining remains.

Illustrations on pages 65–80 have been lent by Desert Designs.

CONTENTS

ACKNOWLEDGMENTS

This exhibition, in simultaneously presenting the work of Jimmy Pike and Desert Designs, explores the key aspects of the artist's own creative path and the interlinking of his aesthetic practice in the evolution of the Fremantle-based company Desert Designs. The engagement of artists in the arena of applied arts is neither new nor incompatible with maintaining an integrity of artistic vision and practice. The story of human aesthetic expression has, from its very beginnings, always been as much about decorating the body through clothing and other body adornment, and enhancing the domestic/urban site through architecture and decorative material culture, as it has been about two-dimensional painting. The transposition of Jimmy Pike's distinctive art work into the fashion and domestic arenas should therefore be seen as part of this larger history, where the formulations of artistic expression have occurred in many forms and settings. The uniqueness lies in the successful collaborative interaction between Jimmy Pike and Desert Designs and in the positive public response that has transformed its tentative beginnings into a recognised national and international design mark over a fifteen-year period.

In closely following the development of this collaboration I have found it both a fascinating story and a rare testament to an enduring personal friendship between Jimmy Pike, David Wroth and Stephen Culley. From the relative isolation of Perth, Desert Designs' development of its national and international profile has shown great initiative and dogged belief in an artist's vision. In turn the artist has placed great faith in the partners' capacity to present his vision with integrity. The worlds of art, fashion and business are notoriously fickle, and the fluctuations of the latter during a decade of rapid change have tested the quality of the collaborative vision through many ups and downs. In working on this exhibition it has therefore been a great pleasure to be closely involved with the artist and his wife, Pat Lowe, as with Stephen Culley and David Wroth, who have all given generously of their time and supported the development of the project as well as lending art works, photographs and other material for inclusion in the exhibition. I extend my sincere thanks to them all for this assistance.

In the exhibition preparation and research, substantial assistance and enthusiasm have been provided by Tjalaminu Mia (née Deborah Eldridge), Curatorial Assistant, whose own work involvement in the early 1980s with the educational programme at Fremantle prison has added additional insight into the time and culture of the period. Many other people have provided information on various aspects of the early Fremantle period and to these and the private lenders of works to the exhibition I also extend my thanks.

I would also like to thank Gallery photographer Greg Woodward and designer Trevor Vincent for their professional input into the critical production process of the catalogue, and Allan Watson for his usual invaluable editorial input. On behalf of the Gallery I would also like to recognise the vital support to the exhibition through the sponsorship of the Lotteries Commission of Western Australia. This has been a vital ingredient in ensuring its successful development and presentation.

Michael O'Ferrall
Curator of Aboriginal and Asian Art

JIMMY PIKE: IMAGE AND APPLICATION

Michael O'Ferrall

The 1980s was an important period in the history of Australian art, it being a decade during which Aboriginal artists of all persuasions began energetically to engage in the mainstream forum of Australian contemporary culture. The impact of the veritable explosion of new Aboriginal artists onto the scene during this time can be seen in their growing representation in permanent public art collections around the country, the number of commercial exhibitions in mainstream galleries and the progressive interest shown internationally. Perhaps one of the most important aspects of these developments has been the emergence of artists from regional areas where strong Aboriginal socio-political movements have brought about a powerful renaissance of cultural identity and consolidation of a new spirit of community.

In Western Australia, one such movement has emerged in the Kimberley, transcending the invisibility of isolation and projecting a re-invigorated sense of its distinctive Aboriginal heritage onto a national stage. This movement has also established a significant Aboriginal presence in many international centres, and, as the realities of the global village continue to unfold, these new inter-cultural connections will undoubtedly strengthen and evolve. On a national front, the emergence of Kimberley artist Jimmy Pike and his collaborative role in the development of Desert Designs represent an important strand in the evolution both of Aboriginal artists' contributions to Australian culture and in their engagement in new opportunities made available by the changing nature of international commercial and cultural interchange.

Jimmy Pike's prints and paintings of the physical and spiritual quality of his traditional Walmajarri Great Sandy Desert country have, since the early 1980s, added a new dynamism to the continuing central position of landscape in Australian art. Simultaneously they project a new dimension to connections of place and identity. The artist's work, with its themes of the intimate intricacies of his desert's landscape, the visual character of the changing seasons and the particularities of its Aboriginal spirituality, has transformed this almost invisible and extremely isolated area of the northern part of the continent into a tangible experience and a rare encounter with both its beauty and its sacredness.

From the 1970s, the gradual emergence of paintings from Papunya and, later, other Central Desert regions has revealed a new face to a hitherto unknown part of Australia. The work of these artists has been instrumental in profoundly transforming earlier cultural projections of the 'Dead Centre' into an understanding of the reality of a previously hidden Aboriginal history and culture of great inventiveness and depth. In a similar fashion, Jimmy Pike (along with Rover Thomas, Jarinyanu David Downs, Peter Skipper and Paddy Tjamitji) has contributed a new vision of and insight into the Kimberley desert and other desert regions adjacent to it. Pike has also, in the development of his distinctive colour and line, created a dimension that, in the freewheeling public area of design, fashion and applied art, has enabled a significant new development in Australian fashion and commercial product application of Aboriginal art and design through his collaboration with Desert Designs.

The philosophy and direction of Desert Designs since its beginnings in 1985 have carried Jimmy Pike's vision well beyond the limitations of 'tourist art' in both application and content. The extension of Desert Designs from a locally based business into a participant in national and inter-national forums has pioneered a new and effective Australian interaction with the global industrial design environment. At the same time it has demonstrated that an artist's individual vision and oevre can be spread to an extremely wide audience through innovative approaches and responses to changing situations in both artistic prac-tice and new readings of cultural definitions.

Beginnings

Given the profound changes that have occurred in the Kimberley and neighbouring desert areas of Western Australia it is not to be expected that the artist Jimmy Pike would have emerged from a conventional art background or that his painting would fit easily into mainstream contemporary art. For much of its last hundred years of history, this isolated region of northern Australia existed as a shifting frontier of uncharted cultural contact between its original Aboriginal inhabitants and newly arrived European explorers, gold miners and cattle men. While the incursion of the first two were of relatively brief duration, the impact of the last resulted in the expansion of a permanent network of cattle stations gradually taking over lands that had previously existed exclusively as the domestic and hunting domains of its many Aboriginal tribal inhabitants.

For much of this time, especially from the late nineteenth century to well into the twentieth century, relationships between these new immigrants and Aborigines were distinguished by periods of fluctuating misunderstanding, new opportunities and violence, both casual and institutionalised through use of police. Resistance consistently indicated the Aboriginal people's fierce attachment to the land, and imprisonment both in local jails and many thousands of kilometres further south on Rottnest Island was common in the early days.

A combination of coercion and the desire for European material goods brought Aborigines to the cattle stations, and the early twentieth century Kimberley beef industry was heavily dependent on Aboriginal stockmen and Aboriginal women working as domestics and cooks. The more inhospitable areas beyond the open valleys and plains of the Kimberley river country were, however, unsuitable for pastoralism. As a consequence, some Aboriginal tribal groups experienced relatively little contact with Europeans until well into the twentieth century. Within the Great Sandy Desert, and further south and east, only the isolated Billiluna cattle station and the Catholic mission settlement of Balgo Hills, established in 1937, brought any significant European presence.

It was thus the case that for Jimmy Pike and other Walmajarri people living in the Great Sandy Desert until the 1950s, the history of black–white contact passed by with relatively little impact on their lives. Harsh by any standards, the desert landscape had nonetheless become the background to a sustainable lifestyle developed by the Walmajarri people and other Central Desert Aboriginal groups over thousands of years.

Above all else, water was central to this lifestyle. The rainy season storms sweeping in from the northern coastal areas provided not only life-sustaining water, but a wide range of plants exploitable for tools and food as well as an environment for animal and bird life. In Walmajarri language and culture the many different sources of water are divided into distinct categories, from *jumu* (temporary soaks), to shallow salt pans that held a few months of fresh rain until it evaporated, to *jila* (permanent wells). This variety of water sources supported an established pattern of shifting camp sites responding to the seasonal changes but able to support family groups and larger ceremonial and initiation gatherings. The frequent appearance of the *Japingka* waterhole (a particular permanent well of ground water) in the artist's works (pages 18, 19, 37, 50, 51) signifies both the physical and spiritual importance that water had for the daily and cultural life of Walmajarri people and for Pike in particular. Spiritually, a Walmajarri person is attached to a particular *jila*. These important sources of water are also imbued with great cultural importance and are associated with *Kalpurtu,* powerful spirits characterised as snakes.

Jilji – the rolling sand dunes that stretch across much of the Great Sandy Desert – also frequently appear in Jimmy Pike's prints and paintings and their general patterning is a central motif in Walmajarri art traditions, for example etched in specific meander patterns into *jakuli* (men's ceremonial pearl shells) and in body painting designs. Like the Central Desert Pintubi and Warlpiri people, whose 'dot and circle' paintings now represent a modern, accessible paradigm for the more complex relationship between art, lifestyle, landscape and Aboriginal spirituality, Jimmy Pike's Walmajarri aesthetic and spiritual roots are firmly based on key visual and life-sustaining features. The Walmajarri people's traditional landscape is a layering of surfaces combining intimately detailed tangible features, imbued with profound and powerful spiritual dimensions created through the activities of the great founding spirits that lived in the Dreamtime.

In the major and often rapid transformations of lifestyle and culture experienced by Jimmy Pike and the other last desert-living Walmajarri people who joined relatives at Cherrabun cattle station in the mid-1950s, their experience of the Great Sandy Desert provided a lasting and profound connecting memory. This knowledge has been carried forward into the changing lifestyles and socio-economic transformations experienced in the Kimberley in the four subsequent decades, and it remains a potent emotional and psychic focus for identity and social cohesion.

This knowledge and traditional experience also supported the small but vital commercial artefact and craft producing industry that Jimmy Pike and other Kimberley artists such as Peter Skipper and Jarinyanu David Downs became involved in at Fitzroy Crossing in the 1970s. This time was a further critical period of great disruption and social insecurity for many Kimberley Aboriginal people, when (in what must be one of the region's most ironic events) the majority of Aboriginal families, who had sustained a living on the network of cattle stations for so long, were made redundant subsequent to a 1968 national landmark industrial award granting equal pay to Aboriginal pastoral industry workers.

An understanding of these historical and recent events – albeit very briefly covered here and details of which are only now emerging through Aboriginal autobiographies – is critical to an appreciation of Jimmy Pike and other Kimberley artists, and a prerequisite to grasping the deep-seated source of their individual artistic visions. Within the wider scope of contemporary Australian art, which until the 1980s could find little common ground with Aboriginal artistic expression, there existed no theoretical precedents or aesthetic models to encompass these dramatic and disruptive experiences. Implicit in Euro-American Modernism, introduced later into Australian art, was the rejection of tradition and the centring on a highly person-alised and innovative (and often purposefully challenging) approach to creative expression. In the particularities of the Australian experience, however, and especially within the dramatic disruptions to Aboriginal customs and beliefs and the interaction with a dominating invasive culture, the themes of continuity and change represent not mutually exclusive domains but essentially connected (if often antagonistic) sources of experience from which to create a coherent single ground. The particular historical and socio-economic changes that Aboriginal people had progressive-ly experienced since British invasion in 1788 were experien-tial features outside this dominant imported intellectual paradigm. The responses of artists like Jimmy Pike are therefore grounded in circumstances and intellectual inten-tions running counter to the dominant culture narrative.

Jimmy Pike, and other Aboriginal artists with similar his-torical and regional experiences, necessitate new critical categories that not only are particular to an Aboriginal experience but reflect the nuances of local histories and personalised experiences. Confronted by often profoundly disruptive events, Pike nonetheless responded by project-ing an extraordinary sense of continuity, fashioning a coherent aesthetic out of the disparate elements of his own experiences.

The emergence of Jimmy Pike as a painter within Fremantle prison is part of this experiential pathway, which, from his leaving the Great Sandy Desert as a young teenager, has led along unexpected and unorthodox path-ways. According to Steve Culley, who was teaching art in the prison in 1980, Pike quickly became an enthusiastic member of the class, and his first Textacolour works on paper and paintings, completed in 1981, reveal avid experi-mentation and speedy mastery of new media. Despite the non-traditional nature of these materials, Pike's output was substantial. He worked with acrylic paint, oil pastel and Textacolour, the last two allowing him to explore and perfect the high colour range that has become his hallmark. The underlying focus and subject matter of his inspiration,

however, rested with a tenacious exploration and re-interpretation of his distant traditional landscape. There is also a strong sense of re-working and extending the para-meters of traditional Walmajarri design elements. Despite the predominance of the figurative South-West 'Carrolup' landscape style practiced by other Aboriginal participants in these art classes, Jimmy Pike showed little inclination to follow this stylistic path.

From the store of Dreamings learnt first as a child in the desert and later enhanced through initiation received from older Walmajarri men while on Cherrabun station, Pike began to set out a wide body of imagery. In the absence of a strong figurative dimension existing within Walmajarri aesthetic – except perhaps in the sense of the three-dimen-sional aspects of ceremonial dance/body decoration – the elements of figuration that Pike developed at this time must be regarded as coming entirely from his own imagi-nation. In the absence of pre-existing schematisation, the artist's early work ranged across both human and animal forms, related through the magical transformational events of the earliest founding period of the Dreamtime itself. In some cases these forms were surrounded by the appropri-ate Walmajarri symbolic designs; in other cases Pike began to focus entirely on stylised landscape references such as falling rain, sand dunes and rocky outcrops.

The black-and-white lino prints made in the prison period (and subsequently produced as silk screened editions due to the fragility of the lino under printing press conditions) reveal the pure graphic element of Pike's work, separated from his use of colour. In developing a ground of subject matter, these prints contain considerable range: from a print such as *Purnara*, based on traditional incised patterns appearing on ceremonial pearl shells used during Walmajarri ceremonies, to figurative compositions based on Dreamtime stories. Recent events are represented in other works, tying together personal reminiscences and critical moments of cultural contact, for example *Jarlujangka Wangki*.

The showing of these prints in the later exhibitions of Pike's work (e.g. December 1984, Praxis Gallery), and sub-sequent publications, have tended to create an impression of progression from line drawing/linocut to later use of colour on paper and on canvas. In fact, Pike did not start working in linocut until the establishment of a print-making facility in the prison art class by David Wroth in 1982/83, but many of his sketches produced in prison were drawn entirely in black Textacolour.

The first few exhibitions of prisoners' art between 1982 and 1983, included works by Pike in Textacolour, crayon and oil

pastel on paper, and in acrylic on canvas. A revisiting of
these works reveals not only the artist's great output from
the time of his joining the prison art classes, but an early
and avid exploration of colour. In a painting such as the
1984 *Sandhills in the Simpson Desert*, the characteristic high
contrast colour banding becomes an abstract exercise in
colour as well as a formal statement of the rhythmic flow
and sense of limitless spaciousness of the desert sand
dunes. This painting was inspired by the artist's chance
viewing of a photograph of this particular desert, which,
though located over a thousand kilometres to the south-
east of the Great Sandy Desert, has close similarities to the
rows of orange-coloured *jilji* (sand ridges) in Pike's familiar
desert homeland.

The production of the first edition of Jimmy Pike's colour
screen prints, exhibited at the Black Swan Gallery in 1986,
revealed a distinct compositional shift from his earlier
black-and-white lino block series, bringing for the first time
a full focus to his love of colour. Produced from original
paintings on paper, they established Pike's reputation as a
colourist, but one with an incisive capacity to stretch to the
point of almost total abstraction the essential linear quali-
ties of the desert landscape. Whether in depicting a specific
waterhole (*Two Men at a Waterhole, Jumangkarni*) or more
panoramic scapes such as (*Larripuka*) and (*Jilji, Yuka, Partiri*),
the allusions to actual landscape features are pared down
to dramatic exercises in pure colour. Subsequent editions of
colour prints in 1987, 1988 and 1989 were drawn from
acrylic, oil pastel and Textacolour works completed while
in prison. The use of near-fluorescent colours in some of
these limited edition prints appeared at the time to be
pushing the use of colour almost to its extreme. However,
the screen prints closely match the intensity of the
originals.

In several subsequent curated exhibitions of works by
Aboriginal artists from around Australia, the paintings
of Ginger Riley Munduwalawala and Sambo Burra from
Ngukurr in south-east Arnhemland showed similar
dramatic use of strong colour, and Pike's work was perhaps seen in a wider comparative perspective than it had
been previously. The appearance of paintings from the
Central Desert community of Yuendumu around the same
time (1986/87) also introduced a dramatically increased
colour range compared with the more muted Papunya
painters' palette, which had closely approximated the traditional coloured ochres. With their bright yellows, blues and
purples, the Yuendumu paintings provided an additional
critical push to the acceptance of the contemporary face of
desert artists, whose early work had been trapped in a critical anthropological time warp, and, with a few exceptions
such as in the Art Gallery of New South Wales' 'Australian

Perspecta 1983', was still regarded with high suspicion by
mainstream critics and commentators on contemporary art.

At this time, the paintings of other Kimberley artists such
as Paddy Tjamitji, Rover Thomas and Jarinyanu David
Downs were beginning to emerge. As prints and paintings
by these artists and Jimmy Pike were exhibited more
widely by commercial galleries in Melbourne, Sydney and
Adelaide, it became more apparent that unconventional
cross-cultural experiences and distinctive regional backgrounds were producing an extraordinarily diverse range
of Aboriginal artistic expression. Simultaneously, a new
range of art-school-trained Aboriginal painters, print-
makers and photographers were beginning to introduce
a separate but equally challenging option as compared
to older notions of what constituted an indigenous
contemporary aesthetic.

While art from the Kimberley and Ngukurr had been treat-
ed with some puzzlement by reviewers and gallery visitors
alike, in the many exhibitions curated in 1987 and 1988,
during the veritable explosion of Australian cultural self-
reviewing in the Bicentennial year it was the 'off centre'
paintings of Jimmy Pike, Robert Campbell Jnr, Rover
Thomas and Ginger Riley Munduwalawala that spoke
most strongly of individual minds at work and best sym-
bolised the emergence of a significant new independent
Aboriginal cultural voice. With their idiosyncratic compositions and perspectives, these works extended a new
bridge across the gulf between the present and the past.
It is perhaps interesting to consider that none of these
artists was particularly young, an orthodox prerequisite
of intellectual innovation.

Stephen Muecke, in his comments on Jimmy Pike's 1987
Crafts Council Gallery show in Sydney, somewhat dryly
observed that the artist's involvement with Desert Designs
allowed him 'to escape the confines of museums, of the
timeless dreaming and government grants'. Pike visited
Sydney to attend the opening of this exhibition, then spent
most of the remainder of the 1980s at Kurlku, located on
the edge the Great Sandy Desert, where he renewed his
acquaintance with the desert, its minute seasonal changes
and its myriad spiritual significances. This period coincid-
ed with an intensive concentration on painting, but he also
continued to draw in Textacolour. The two versions of
Partiri – Desert Flowers (pages 64/65) produced during
this time are evidence of a significant development from
the landscapes drawn from memory while he was in
Fremantle. Their delicacy and kaleidoscopic brilliance are
a striking counter to the notions of a harsh lifeless desert
and a stylistic departure from the solid banded colours of
his earlier colour prints.

His appearance in several group exhibitions consistently demonstrated the strength of his vision in a wide range of artistic company. This exposure also enabled a wider critical grasp of his inspiration, and resulted in a better comparative understanding of the particularities of the Aboriginal character of the Kimberley region. Pike's inclusion in exhibitions alongside artists such as Rover Thomas and David Jarinyanu Downs extended the growing public understanding of the richness of its cultural and physical character and provided a comparative forum in which to contrast the different view of each of these artists. This also enabled a better grasp of the nexus of design and culture as developed within the Desert Designs operation.

The release of new prints series in 1991 showed the results of Pike's three years on the edge of the Great Sandy Desert. Many of these were directly based on studies of the landscape, revealing an enhanced, direct sense of perspective absent from earlier work. The daily contact with the desert's extended vistas, changing seasonal colours and vegetation led to them being more directly featured in these prints. A separate thread, dealing with the Dreamtime beings of the Walmajarri landscape, was also evident in both his paintings and his prints. *Kuntumaru* and *Parnaparnti*, two important Walmajarri ancestral beings, figured frequently in both mediums, indicating, perhaps, the powerful psychological impact of the artist's renewal with his landscape and its mythological associations. Related directly to Pike's special waterhole at *Japingka*, these two beings are constantly re-explored in different ways, and at different points of the great Dreaming narrative which links them from the Great Sandy Desert all the way to the coastal regions of Broome. Separately from the dominant figurative images, the artist also moved to compositions that were intensely abstract and showed a more subtle tonality of colour than was evident in his earlier prints. Since he moved to Broome many of his paintings appear to have followed this artistic direction, with its use of a narrower range of colour. The result is a very sparse, refined appearance.

At this point in time the artist is also centrally involved with the development of Walmajarri land claim matters as a result of the ground-breaking High Court Mabo ruling. As a senior figure in his tribal group, Pike, along with artist Peter Skipper and other elders at Fitzroy Crossing, is responsible for confirming and identifying the critical cultural map of the Great Sandy Desert. Throughout his artistic career this close relationship with his land incorporating the intricate associations with its physical character and spiritual meaning, have remained the central inspirational force in his artmaking. From the time that he first left the desert in the early 1950s to the present day, many changes have taken place, but his art and his personal engagement with the landscape have refused to be diminished by them. Rather, they have intensified and strengthened, and, through his own visionary contribution, have maintained the sense of the essential continuous present encapsulated in the bond between Aborigines and their land.

Desert Designs

Stephen Culley and David Wroth had shared art interests in Perth during the early 1970s and had been friends since early childhood. Their friendship was consolidated in 1977 when they travelled to the Kimberley region of the far north of Western Australia. There they camped and moved around the area in an old secondhand car and painted the landscape during most of the year. Like many other emerging artists they were intent on extending their own skills and subject matter and benefiting from first-hand experience. Of the many available areas in the vastness of the state, they were drawn to the Kimberley region by its distance from the overworked Perth urban landscape. By inclination they were also seeking an alternative to the 'conceptual' theories prevalent at art school during Culley's undergraduate years: a time when intellectuals and many teachers were questioning the very foundations of art production and when text and 'the empty wall' were features of cutting edge practice.

This experience, though not connected directly with the later development of Desert Designs, nonetheless gave them an important grounding in the Kimberley of the 1970s and the dominant Aboriginal community presence in the small towns of Fitzroy Crossing, Halls Creek, Wyndham and Derby. Most importantly it meant that Culley had a real sense of the region's social and cultural background when, as teacher in charge of Fremantle prison art classes, he first met Jimmy Pike in 1981. There was no specific agenda adopted by Culley in running the classes other than to provide as many opportunities as possible to explore the whole art-making process. In his own words, Culley was in the beginning largely concerned with 'getting enough art materials from the prison authorities and encouraging the widest possible approach to artistic expression' rather than 'teaching any particular style or technique of art'. The diversity of regional backgrounds of those attending the classes meant that a wide range of subject matter and stylistic variations occurred naturally within the class setting. It has been stated several times by Culley that he found Jimmy Pike a spontaneous and eager painter from their first encounters and that he was never sure just who was the teacher and who the student. Even in the first WA prisoners' art exhibition at the Fremantle Arts Centre in

1981, Jimmy Pike's paintings on canvas, Masonite and paper stood out as uncompromising, and their distinctive appearance attracted significant visitor interest and sales.

David Wroth began to teach in the art classes in 1982, when the acquisition of a printing press and other equipment enabled an expansion of media options available to prisoners. In Wroth's classes, Pike began to work on linocuts while he continued to draw in Textacolour pens and paint on paper and canvas. The result was a suite of dramatic prints first exhibited at Praxis Gallery, Fremantle (pages 17–26). By the time of this particular exhibition, both teachers had formed a close friendship with Jimmy Pike and were aware, as artists themselves, of the possible opportunities available to Pike on his discharge.

In the early part of the 1980s, there was little Western Australian Aboriginal art exhibited in Perth. Only the enigmatic Wandjina images from the north and Carrolup South West style landscapes provided any evidence of a contemporary face to Aboriginal art. (Nyungar artist Shane Pickett provided an important extension of landscape emphasis on graduating from art school in 1982.) Bark paintings from Arnhemland and Central Desert acrylic paintings were the dominant forms of Aboriginal art exhibited to the Perth public by the only specialist Aboriginal art gallery in the city. In local contemporary terms, the prisoners' art exhibitions from 1981 to 1985 introduced a wide diversity of paintings to a Perth public whose only exposure otherwise to contemporary idioms was through the brightly coloured and stylised South West landscapes of the Carrolup school painters. The appearance of a new community-run Fremantle exhibition space, Birukmarri Gallery, which opened in 1986 in response to an anticipated America's Cup yacht race tourism boom, greatly enhanced the range of Aboriginal art exhibitions in Perth; Jimmy Pike's prints and early Desert Designs clothing became a central feature of their exhibition programme and displays. A second specialist Aboriginal art gallery, Dreamtime Gallery, opened in the same year. Both galleries closed in the late 1980s as a result of a tourist downturn following an airline pilots' strike and the rapid fall in general art sales subsequent to the 1987 stock market crash.

The transposition of Pike's work onto textiles first occurred in 1985. Aboriginal textiles with contemporary designs had been pioneered in the 1970s on Bathurst Island by Tiwi Bima Wear and at Ernabella and Utopia with the production of batik textile lengths. The earliest Pike designs selected for transfer onto cotton were chosen for their combination of strong linear character and colour range. (See pages 33 and 73 for an original painting on paper and the transformation into clothing, also pages 66 and 68.)

The intention in developing the first line of textiles was to jump over the stereotypical 'craft-based' association of individual design and textiles. Instead, Culley and Wroth wanted to generate a product that was would fully interface with the professional, commercial world of contemporary design and fashion without losing the essence of Jimmy Pike's creativity and its Aboriginal cultural integrity. They used local fashion designer Lon Riley and seamstress Nina Boydelle to prepare suitable patterns for their first small range of fashion garments which they sold through individual boutiques around Perth.

In the same year a short article by a freelance journalist appeared in the *Rag Trader*, a national clothing trade magazine based in Sydney. At this time the two partners in the fledgling enterprise had no office or official base, but were operating from Steve Culley's home. Although they were convinced that Jimmy Pike's art fitted directly into the new wave of contemporary idiom that was beginning to emerge in different locations around the country, they were not consciously looking to develop a nationwide mark immediately. But Sydney freelance fashion promoter/organiser Christine Bookallil became interested in the ideas she read about in the *Rag Trader* article and invited Culley and Wroth to contribute Desert Designs products to an Australian promotion planned for the Neiman Marcus department store in the USA later in 1985.

The partners were unable to provide the necessary merchandise in the time available. While on a visit to Sydney, however, to meet with Christine Bookallil, Steve Culley and his brother Darrell, an accountant who had provided the initial seed capital, were introduced to the commercial design licensing process and J. H. Byers' fashion company. After seeing their concept storyboards and Fremantle-produced clothing, Byers expressed interest in licensing specific designs for a range of children's wear and women's fashion, with the first release occurring in the summer of 1986/87. (See pages 70, 71 and 72 for the first winter season line.) Separately, Culley and Wroth had already discussed with Jimmy Pike strategies for developing a career as a full-time artist on his release from prison in 1986. Though isolated in jail, he had already gained some understanding of the commercial aspects of the art world through the several prisoners' art exhibitions and the steady sale of his work. These exhibitions occurred in 1982/83 at His Majesty's Theatre and as part of the 'Aboriginal Arts in Perth '83 Festival' organised by Derek Holroyde, Director of the Centre for Communication and the Arts at what was then the Western Australian Institute of Technology. Successful exhibitions were also held at the Praxis/Nexus arts cooperative galleries in Fremantle in 1984 and 1985.

During 1985 and 1986 Pike entered into a series of business arrangements with Culley and Wroth. These would protect the integrity of his art (and separate the paintings and the production/marketing of limited edition prints) but enable additional income to be derived from the licensing of his designs and the strategic development of the Desert Designs company. Thus, the artist's creative works and inspiration formed both the philosophical and practical foundation of the enterprise as it developed, and they have maintained this central role up to the present day.

Along with the first release of the Byers fashion and fabric range, 1986/87 saw the securing of licensing agreements with national companies Oroton and Sheridan by Desert Designs. The Oroton and Byers concept ranges were a significant step, projecting the Jimmy Pike/Desert Designs concept package into a national mainstream market and establishing a sophisticated connection between the ethos of Aboriginal design and contemporary artistic expression. In Sydney, Bronwyn Bancroft and Laurence Leslie were two other Aboriginal artist/textile designers who were developing similar approaches at this time.

A major step for Desert Designs occurred in 1987. Through a chance personal contact and subsequent assistance from Austrade staff in Tokyo, Desert Designs was able to elicit interest from the Seibu chain of department stores in staging a market-testing promotional display. The result was the opening in August of the 'Jimmy Pike – Desert Designs' exhibition in the gallery space of the Seibu store in the Shibuyu district of Tokyo. The show toured to other Seibu stores across Japan during the following six months.

Steve Culley and David Wroth had not consciously aimed at the Japanese market, but the opportunity offered significant exposure and exponentially expanded their horizons into the international arena. It is interesting and instructive that the Japanese not only took on board the conceptual and cultural aspects of the combination of Pike and Desert Designs, but in designing the exhibition contributed a substantial supporting programme themselves (see page 76 for the poster designed in Japan for the exhibition). Prior to the exhibition opening, Seibu arranged for a group of their artists/display designers to visit Jimmy Pike at his bush camp on the edge of the Great Sandy Desert to produce a documentary video of the landscape. As well as documenting the landscape and collecting ideas for display themes for the forthcoming exhibition the artists themselves produced paintings alongside Pike (page 76). A group of Kimberley Aboriginals also visited Tokyo during the opening and performed traditional dances.

This not only exemplifies the style of commercial operation of Japanese department stores in developing an overseas product for the home market, but suggests that Seibu organisers grasped the essential connection between artistic expression and deeper cultural dimensions inherent in Jimmy Pike's work and carried through in the total concept philosophy espoused by Desert Designs. From its earliest beginnings, the Japanese sense of aesthetic has been concerned with the fusion of form and spirit, surface and inner meaning, and the energy created in the subtle interplay of these outer and inner dimensions. In retrospect, and from a cross-cultural point of view, the perceived contradictions between Aboriginal traditional culture and a contemporary form of expression, often voiced in Australia at that time, were not seen as antagonistic from a Japanese perspective. Rather, in parallel with Japan's own aesthetic history and critical transformations in the Meiji era and post World War II period, tradition and evolution were accepted as integral to any cultural perspective.

This pioneering 1987 exhibition was successful and Seibu organised a second promotional presentation in 1989 and developed licensed designs into a range of merchandise products including ski wear (page 77) and beach wear. In the general mood of this success, and the wider optimism generated by the Australian and global economic growth of the mid to late 1980s, Desert Designs also opened its own stores in Sydney, Surfers Paradise and Fremantle (page 78), where they had established an office in 1986. It was during the later part of 1987 that Jimmy Pike made one of his few interstate trips to attend an exhibition opening, preferring generally to avoid such events. This was at the Rocks Gallery in Sydney. A further consolidation of the company's impact in the fashion industry was realised when Desert Designs women's clothing produced by J. H. Byers' company won the New Talent category of the 1988 Bicentennial Fashion Awards (*Mode*, August/ September, 1988).

The reverberations of the 1987 stock market crash did not impact immediately on Desert Designs, though the 1989 Australian airline pilots' six-month strike was to have a serious effect on their own retailing operations. Fueled by their Japanese experiences and a better understanding of licensing procedures and opportunities, as well as perhaps the profile opportunities offered by separately organised overseas Bicentennial exhibitions of Jimmy Pike's art, the company participated in several international developments. This can be seen as a deliberate new phase in the life of the company. A European office was established in 1989 by Ian Plunkett, a new Director of the company, and from this base new marketing directions were explored.

Between 1991 and 1992 licenses were negotiated with Superba, Unigroup Plc, Copyright, Grangewood, Bomat NV and Mitchelsons. This took place within the framework of a conceptual brand presentation, which included details such as the stories associated with each design in order to reinforce the message of the uniqueness of Pike's design library and its cultural integrity. Other specific developments in this period were the opening of a Desert Designs gallery/shop in Toulouse, France, (1991–1993) and a short-term promotional outlet in Covent Garden, London. Though British company Marks and Spencer showed interest in a large concept merchandise range in 1990, Desert Designs did not sign an agreement with them, considering them to be not in an appropriate market position.

In 1990, Steve Culley established a presence in the USA, licensing merchandising lines with Mitsubishi (USA) and a menswear line through departmental stores like Saks. Montero, haute couture silk designers/manufacturers based in Como, Italy, created a special line of ties for the American market, responding to what they considered to be one of the best design concepts they had seen in many years. In this engagement with the global market, the company consciously sought to project Desert Designs and Jimmy Pike as a new inspiration and new icon of Australian fashion. They presented a total concept that emphasised originality and freshness with a distinctive point of difference. During this time another permanent artist was brought into Desert Designs. Doris Gingingara's art was seen as a fine complement to Jimmy Pike's, adding a woman's story dimension and the influence of Arnhemland coastal culture.

Since 1992 Desert Designs has seen itself entering a third phase, encapsulated in the theme 'Art, Culture, Environment'. This has involved a refinement and a more sophisticated conceptualisation of Desert Designs visual point of difference within a market where dots have become the common currency for Aboriginal aesthetic expression and several commercial enterprises have targeted the tourist market. During the period the company has tightened its control of the design and retail aspects of its operations, opening its own shops and looking for manufacturing opportunities within Australia. Equally, it has built on earlier groundwork and intensified its focus on premier international departmental stores.

In formulating an overall view of the growth and direction of Desert Designs up to the present time, one comes to see that the common feature has been the consistently optimistic approach of Stephen Culley and David Wroth to exploring new ideas and market possibilities. In the commercial world, beyond the vicissitudes of everyday business and the fickleness of market acceptance of distinctive design, the company had retained an open-ended view of market possibilities and global directions. At the same time, the integral connection between Jimmy Pike's vision and Desert Designs has been maintained, in close adherence to the initial concept. The process of integrating art into the commercial marketplace is always prone to be influenced by market forces, which have a tendency to distort or disjoint aesthetic integrity. At this point in time, the collaborative relationship established a decade ago between Jimmy Pike, Stephen Culley and David Wroth has successfully negotiated these pitfalls and established a distinctive chapter not only in the continuing evolution of Kimberley Aboriginal art but in the wider field of Australian fashion, design and applied art.

BIOGRAPHY

Born Great Sandy Desert, WA, 1940

Exhibitions
Aboriginal Artists Gallery, Melbourne, 1985
Aboriginal Artists Gallery, Sydney, 1986
Black Swan Gallery, Fremantle, 1986
Tynte Gallery, Adelaide, 1987
Craft Centre Gallery, Sydney, 1987
Seibu Shibuya, Tokyo, Japan, 1987
Australian Consulate, Hong Kong, 1987
Galerie Exler, Frankfurt, 1987
Addendum Gallery, Fremantle, 1988
Blaxland Galleries, Sydney, 1988
Birukmarri Gallery, Fremantle, 1988
Capricorn Gallery, Port Douglas, 1988
Tynte Gallery, Adelaide, 1988
Blaxland Gallery, Sydney and Melbourne, 1988
Bloomfield Gallery, Sydney, 1989
Australian Embassy, Paris, 1989
Studio-Galerie des Hauses der Kulturen der Welt,
Berlin, 1990
Nolan Gallery, Canberra, 1990
Covent Garden Exhibition, London, 1991
AMS Stores, Japan, 1991
Kimberley Creations, Broome, 1992
Gallery in the Vineyard, Germany, 1993
Caulfield Centre, Melbourne, 1994
Australia Centre, Manila, 1995

Group Exhibitions
'Winds of Change', Nexus Gallery, Fremantle, 1983
(Aboriginal Arts in Perth '83, Festival)
His Majesty's Theatre, Perth, 1982/1984
Praxis Gallery, Fremantle, 1984
(2nd Indian Ocean Arts Festival)
Print Council Gallery, Melbourne, 1987
'A Changing Relationship – Aboriginal Themes
in Aboriginal Art 1938–1988', S. H. Ervin Gallery,
Sydney, 1988
New Tracks, Old Land, Touring USA, 1994

Collections
Represented in
Australian National Gallery, Canberra
Art Gallery of Western Australia, Perth
National Gallery of Victoria, Melbourne
Art Gallery of South Australia, Adelaide
Art Gallery of New South Wales, Sydney
Holmes à Court Collection, Perth
Christensen Fund, Melbourne
Australian Museum, Sydney
Private collections

Commissions
BHP 1987
Mount Newman Mining 1987
Bicentennial Poster, 1988

Publications
Jimmy Pike: His Art and his Stories,
Desert Prints, Perth, 1986
Amadio, N.
Jimmy Pike Graphics
Christensen Fund, Perth, 1988
Beier, U.
Jimmy Pike: bilde aus der Grossen Australischen Sandwuste.
Haus der Kulturen der Welt, Berlin, 1990
Isaacs, J.
Aboriginality
Brisbane, Queensland University Press, 1989
Lowe, P. and Pike, J.
Jilji: Life in the Great Sandy Desert
Broome, Magabala Books, 1990
Lowe, P. and Pike, J.
Yinti: Desert Child
Broome, Magabala Books, 1994

BIBLIOGRAPHY

Kim Ackermann
Riji and Jakuli: Kimberley Pearl Shell in Aboriginal Australia
(Monograph series no. 4)
Darwin, Northern Territory Museum of Arts and Sciences,
1993

Jack Bohemia and William MacGregor
Nyibayarri, Kimberley Tracker
Canberra, Aboriginal Studies Press, 1995

Anne Brodie
*Contemporary Aboriginal Art from the
Robert Holmes à Court Collection* (catalogue)
Perth, Heytesbury Holdings Ltd, 1990

Wally Caruana
*Windows on the Dreaming: Aboriginal Paintings
in the Australian National Gallery*
Sydney, Ellsyd Press, 1989

Wally Caruana
Aboriginal Art
London, Thames & Hudson, 1993

Contemporary Aboriginal Art 1990 from Australia (catalogue)
Sydney, Aboriginal Arts Committee, Australia Council,
and Glasgow, Third Eye Centre, 1990

Patricia Lowe and Jimmy Pike
Jilji: Life in the Great Sandy Desert
Broome, Magabala Books, 1990

Patricia Lowe and Jimmy Pike
Yinti: Desert Child
Broome, Magabala Books, 1993

David Mowaljarlai and Jutta Malnic
Yoro Yoro
Broome, Magabala Books, 1993

Howard Pederson
'Pigeon, an Aboriginal Rebel: A Study of Aboriginal–
European Conflict in the West Kimberley, North Western
Australia During the 1890s', unpublished honours thesis,
Murdoch University, 1980

Judith Ryan
Images of Power: Aboriginal Art of the Kimberley (catalogue)
Melbourne, National Gallery of Victoria, 1993

John E. Stanton
Innovative Aboriginal Art of Western Australia (catalogue)
Perth, The University of Western Australia
Anthropology Research Museum, 1988

John E. Stanton
*Painting the Country: Contemporary Aboriginal Art
from the Kimberley Region, Western Australia* (catalogue)
Perth, The University of Western Australia Press, 1989

Peter Sutton (ed.)
Dreamings: The Art of Aboriginal Australia (catalogue)
Melbourne, Viking, 1989

The Quest for Jimmy Pike (video)
Sydney, Juniper Films, 1990

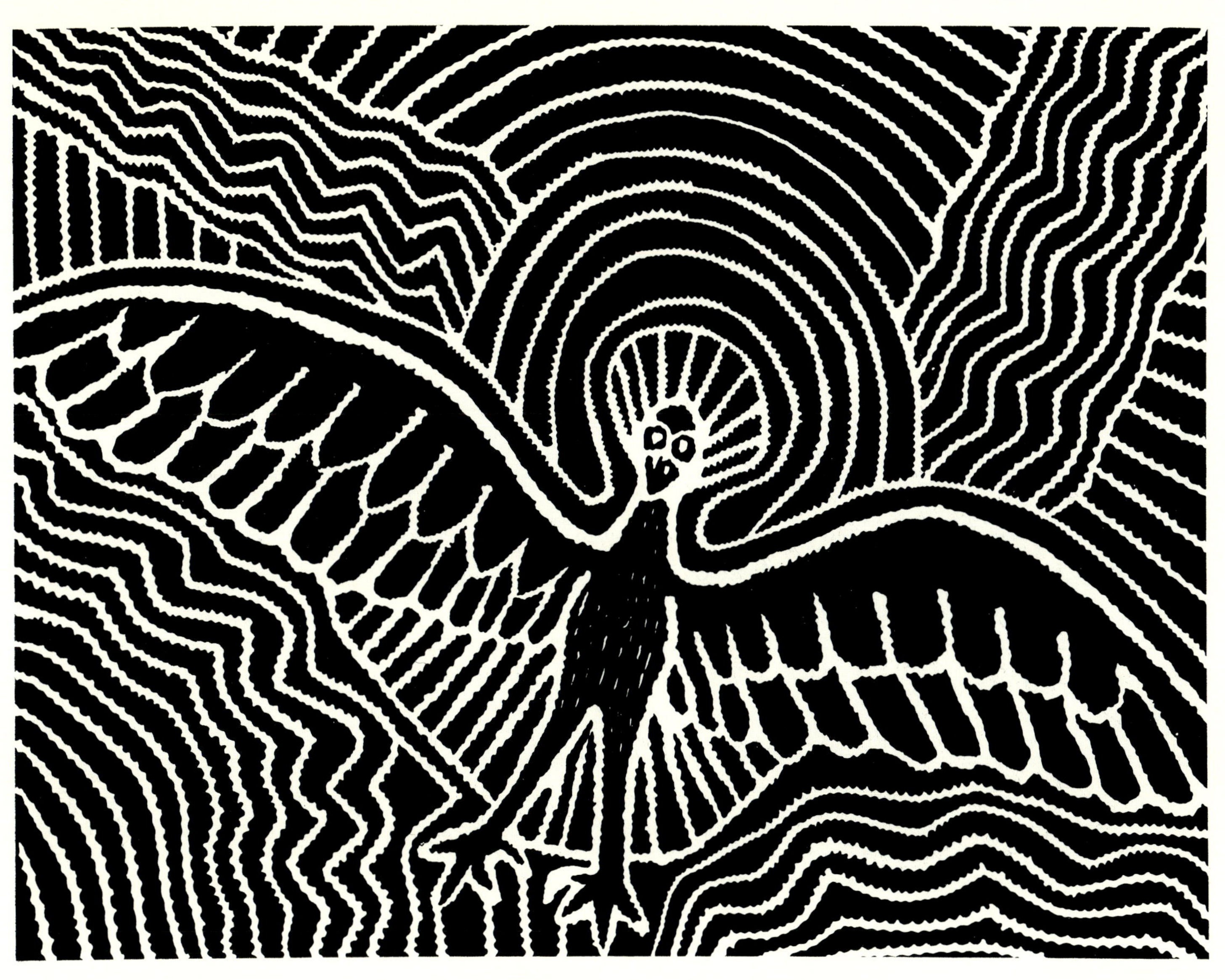

Mangkaja Kura 1984
linocut
34.2 x 44.0 cm
Artist's proof

When he comes down, he sinks down and the ground
sinks down. As he goes down, he goes round in a circle,
and makes steps in the rock right down. People can climb
down the steps when they get water. This is *jilji* [sandhill]
country.

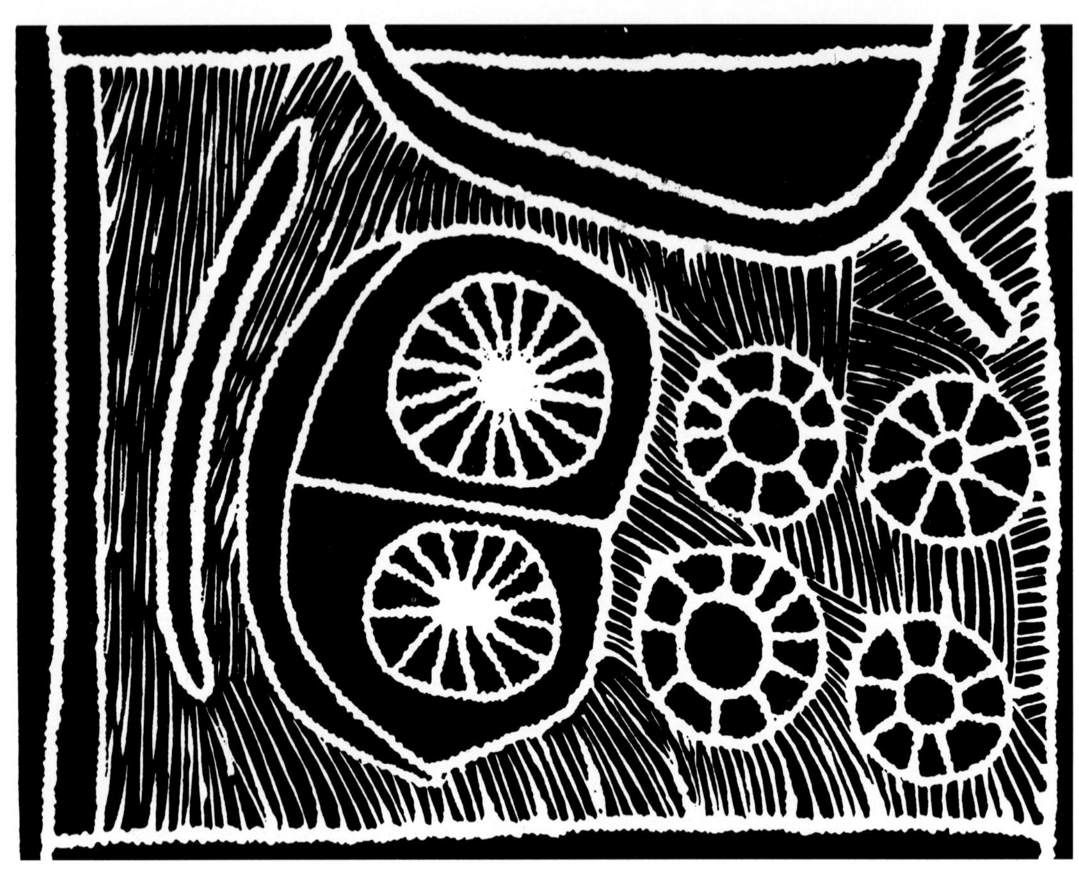

**Japingka Waterhole –
Dreamtime Story II**
1984
linocut
34.1 x 44.3 cm
Artist's proof

Six brothers were living at this place. Two women came here and the six *Pajarriwarnti* brothers were turned into a snake. A big strong wind, a willi-willi, sprung up and dragged them down into the waterhole. The ground grew damp, and clouds came up from the ground. *Ngalyamarra* is the rock ledge around the waterhole. The water comes from deep under the ground. The people gather round the waterhole to tell the snake to bring water. Above the waterhole is a big sandhill where only men can go.

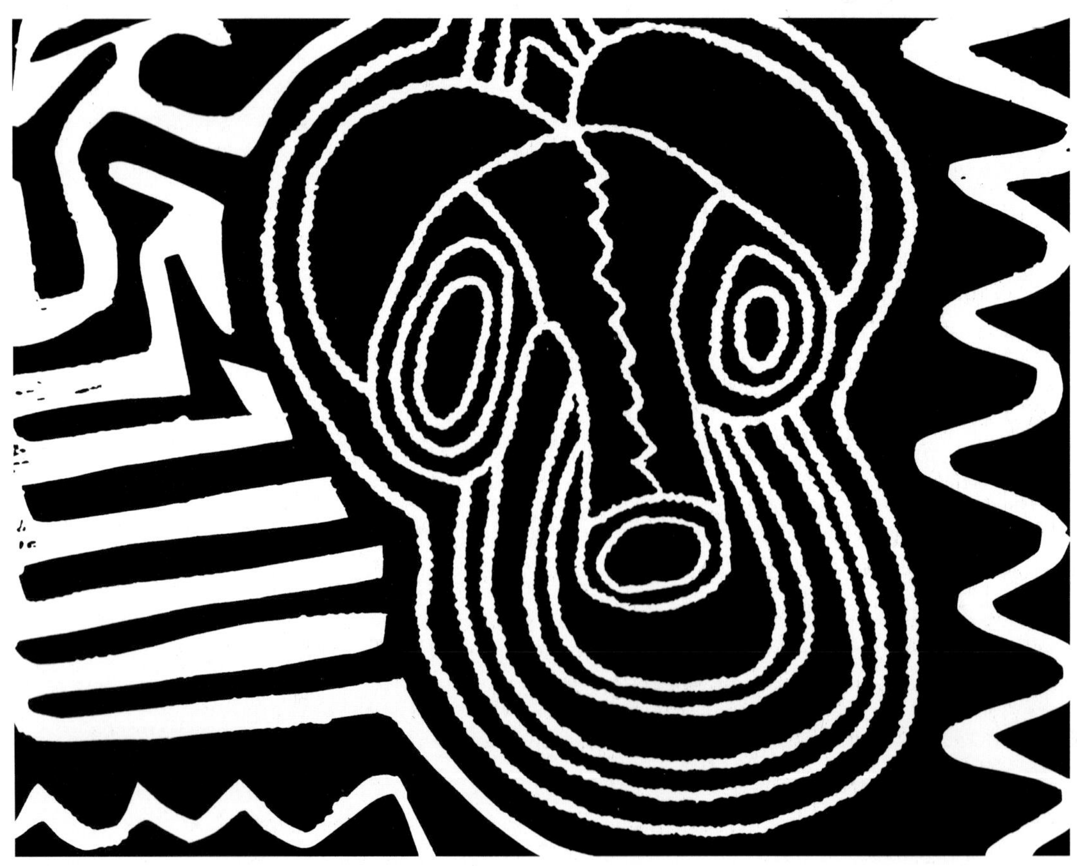

**Two Men Sitting
at a Waterhole** 1984
linocut
32.9 x 44.0 cm
Artist's proof

Two men were sitting each side of a waterhole. This waterhole is *Tingki*. The two men are *Pitingaji* and *Wurta*; they are wild with one another. They are having an argument about the land. They are from different places and they have story problems. They turned into two rocks by this waterhole.

Japingka –
Dreamtime Story I
1985
screenprint
33.8 x 43.5 cm
Edition: 36/85

When people come to the
waterhole, the snake comes
to see what people come.
When people first come to
this place, they take mud
and rub it all over their
bodies. After that they
become friendly with the
water snake. The snake at
Japingka knows everything
that goes on here.

Warnti 1985
screenprint
31.6 x 43.0 cm
Edition: 26/95

The people go from one
jila [waterhole] to another.
Japingka is the main *jila*. This
one is *Warnti* waterhole.
Warnti live a long time at this
waterhole. People been coming here more than 20,000
years. The people gone, but
the water is still there.
Something keep the water
there – snake. He keeps the
waterhole. These big trees,
ngarlka grows around the
banks of the *Warnti*. Their
roots keep the water. When
one tree dies another grows
back in its place. *Ngalyamarra*
is the white rock by this
waterhole. It keeps the water
cold. This is *ngapa* drinking
water. The water comes up
through the bank, from
underground. This is
surrounded by sandhills.

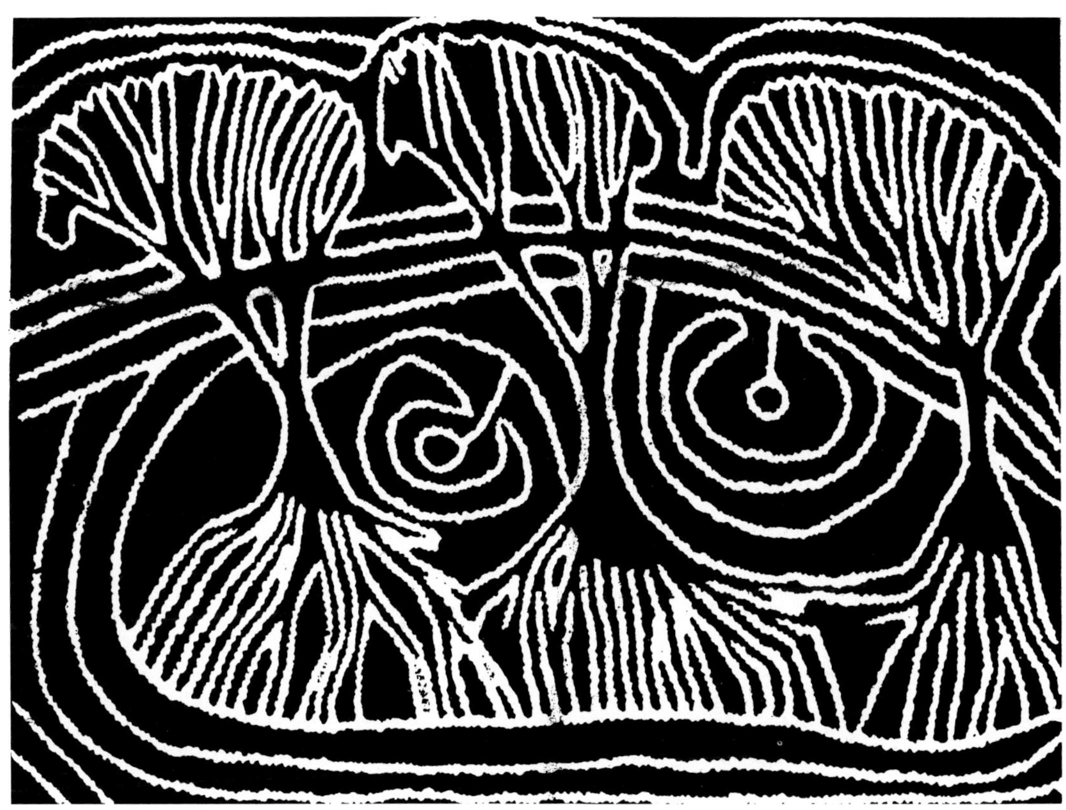

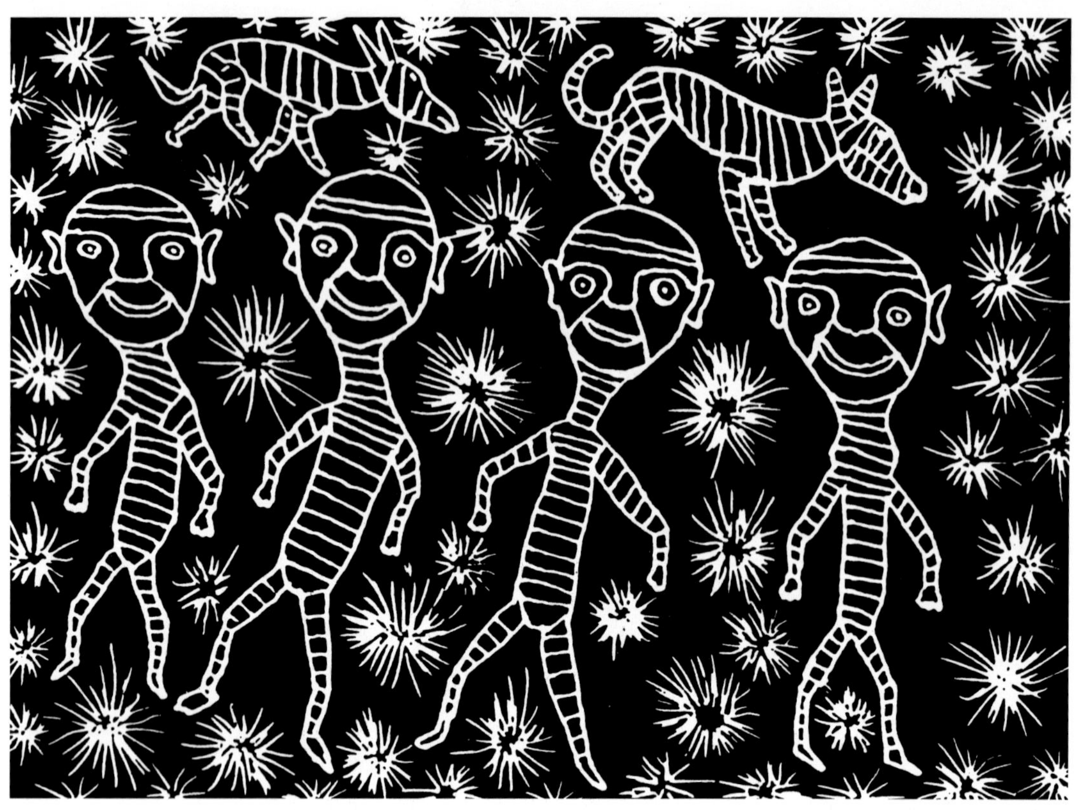

Murungurrwarnti 1985
screenprint
33.0 x 45.0 cm
Edition: 54/80

Little men, they live in hill and scrub country or near *jila* [waterhole]. They look like watersnakes. They don't like strangers. They can make people sick. They fight over honey. If you find a big mob of honey, fill up your billy-can, they will come out and fight you, give you a good hiding. You can't see them or feel them, but after, when you drink water, you see the lumps on your body.

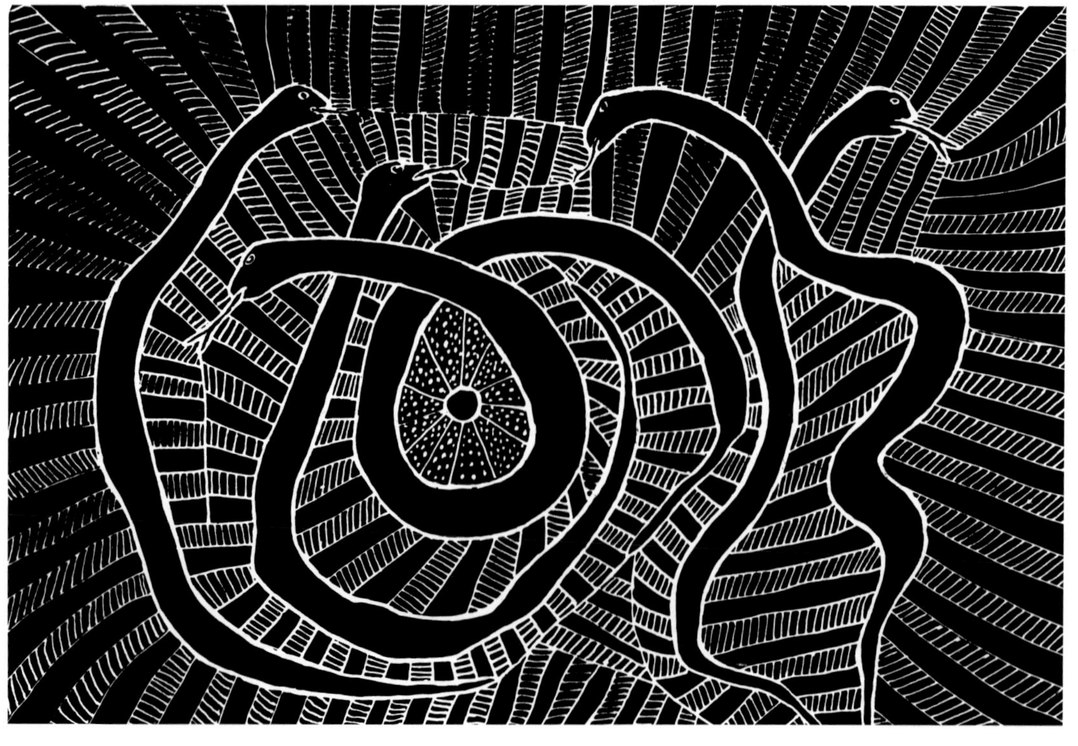

Warnajiljikarraji 1985
screenprint
30.2 x 45.0 cm
Edition: 72/85

Snake living in the sand-hills. It eats sand and lives in a hole. When big mob come in, they make smooth tracks going round. Sometimes they might fight over a female snake. Sometimes the female run away, leaves them fighting.

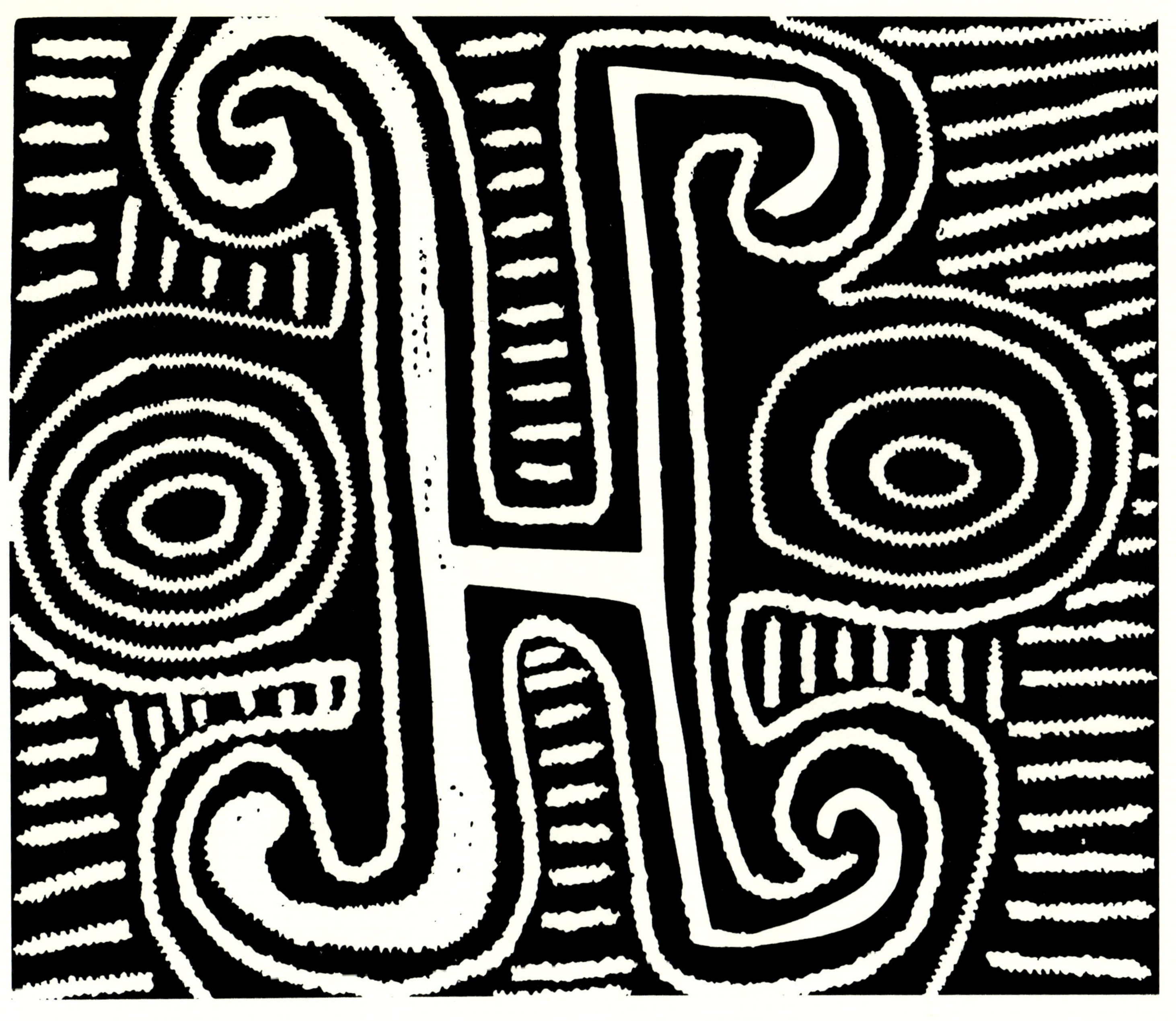

Two Men Sleeping by Two Fires 1985
screenprint
31.5 x 37.6 cm
Edition: 45/85

These two old men are sleeping by two fires. They
have made a windbreak all around and are curled up.
They are cousin-brothers, *Parnaparnti* and *Kurntumaru*.
Kurntumaru is the black goanna that hides in trees.
Parnaparnti is the yellow sand goanna.

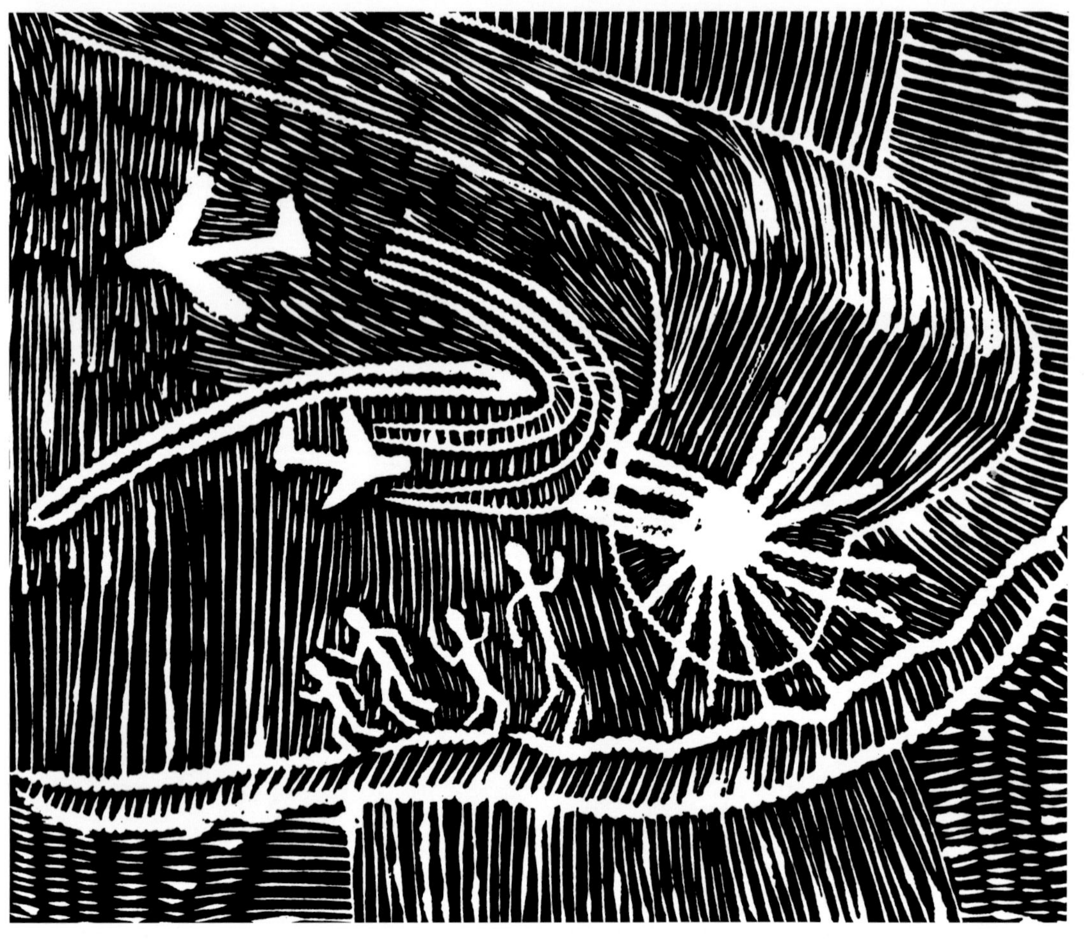

Jarlujangka Wangki
1985
screenprint
33.0 x 39.3 cm
Edition: 31/85

Old time story, not Dreamtime. People story – real one. This is a real story. One day they went hunting near this waterhole. My father went over to Canning Stock Route with other wife, left mother and little sister at waterhole. One day they went hunting from waterhole. They make bushfire in thick grass, spinifex. Make big fire, burn big, stand at edge. Little kangaroo and goanna run out. Then they hear noise like dragonfly at swamp. Plane come right into fire and drop something [a bomb] on fire. Mother and children hide under bush and tree. They went back to waterhole. Then they come back they find that place, they find bits of tin from that thing. Still there today.

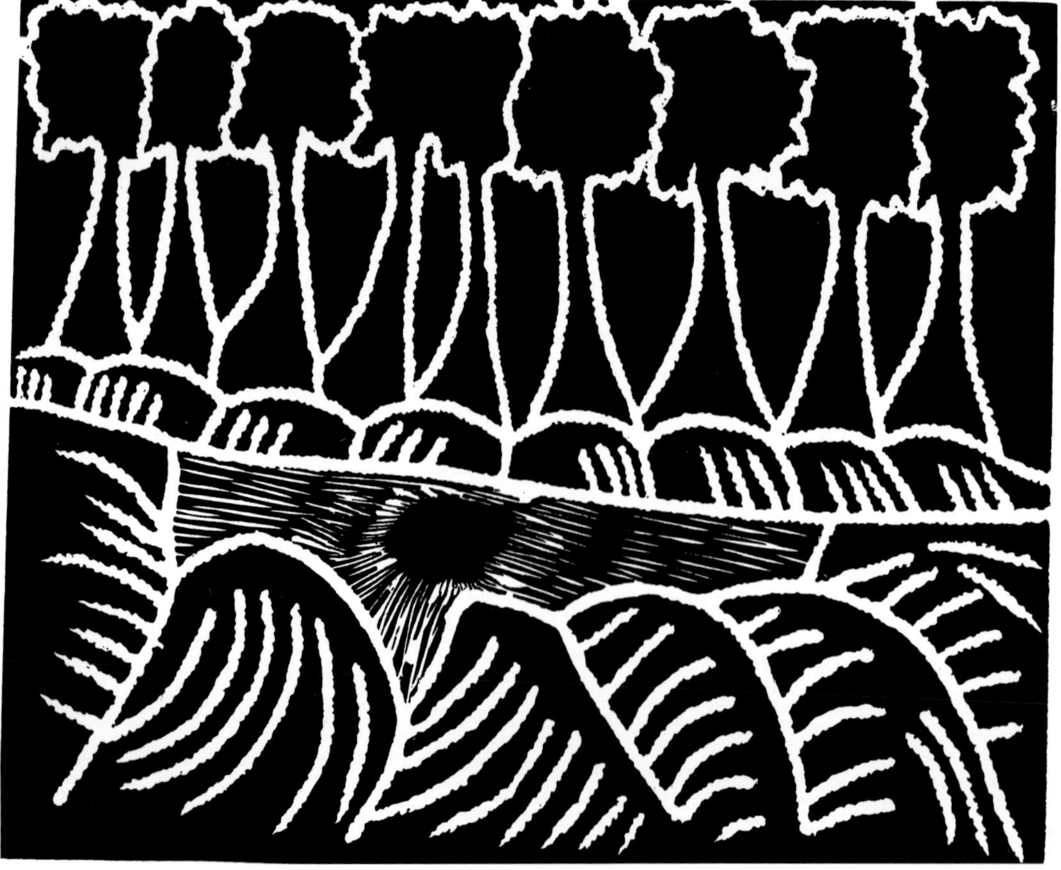

Billabong Karru 1985
screenprint
32.8 x 41.0 cm
Edition: 30/50

People come back from hunting to this waterhole – named *Karru*. Like a creek. Plenty *Karru* in my country.

Purnara 1985
screenprint
34.0 x 42.3 cm
Edition: 56/75

Purnara – this marking is like a number, a brand. It is used by the Aboriginal people over a big area. It shows that anything with this mark comes from the bush-desert south of Kimberleys. When people see this *purnara* carving, they know what number that country has. 'Ah, that come from my country.' Many tribes use the same number, same meaning, cut different way. Carving on *nulla nulla* (spear), *woomera* (shield), *coolamon* (water holder), *marrilaly* (shovel for cooking), *wangkuli* (pan for wheat), *tarta* (cup).

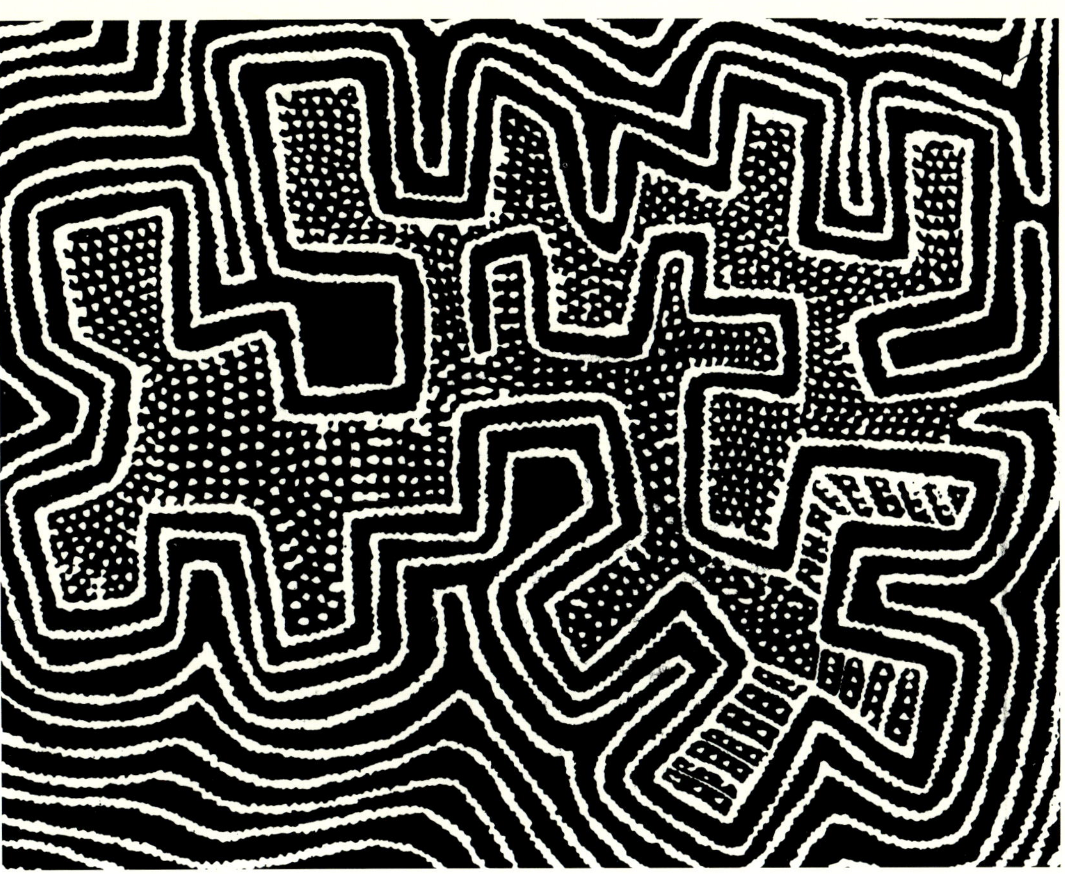

Mirnmirt 1985
screenprint
32.3 x 42.3 cm
Edition: 7/45

When single woman like a man, she draw this story in the mud with a stick. When woman talk about a man, talks about love, she draws this story. When someone tells, or a man sees a story, then he goes to the woman. Then they talk marriage. *Mirnmirt* is marriage law. When man has finished the law, done everything, he can marry. He has got to learn everything. There are two laws. One for the young boy takes several months. One for the full man takes five or six years. When man come back from bush after manhood, woman sitting. They have a big feast and make man and woman red with clay.

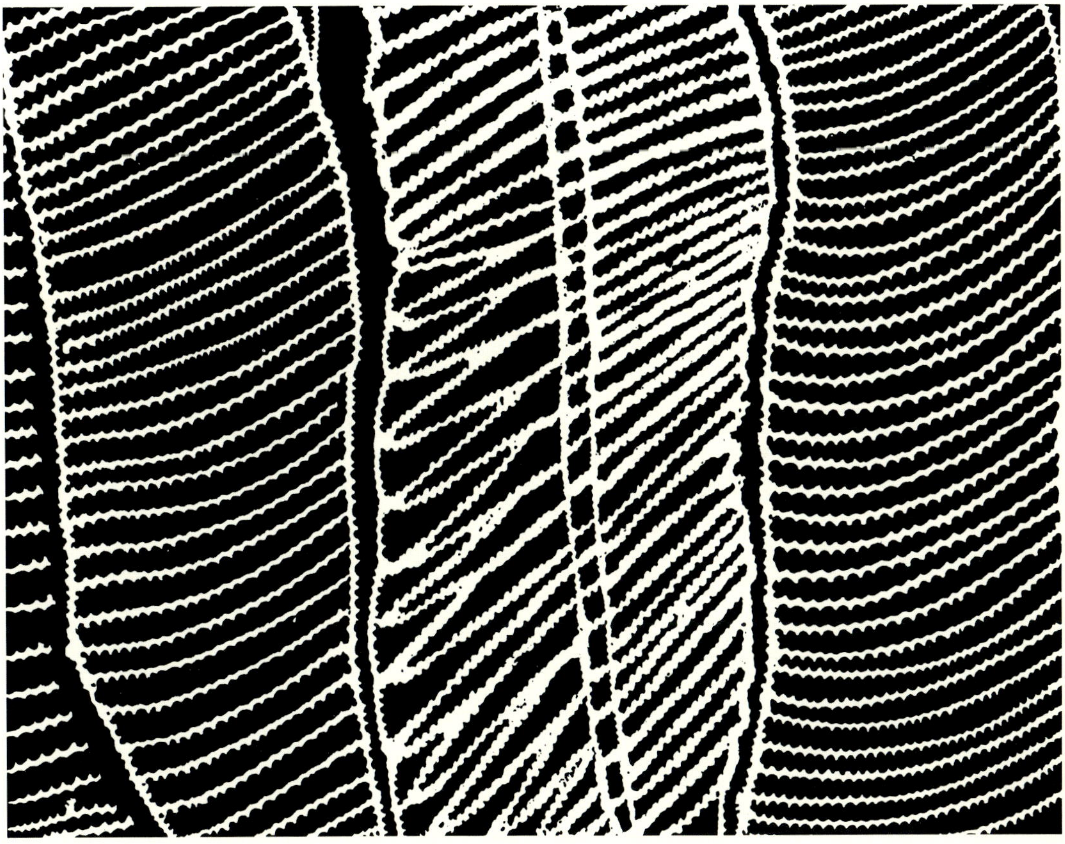

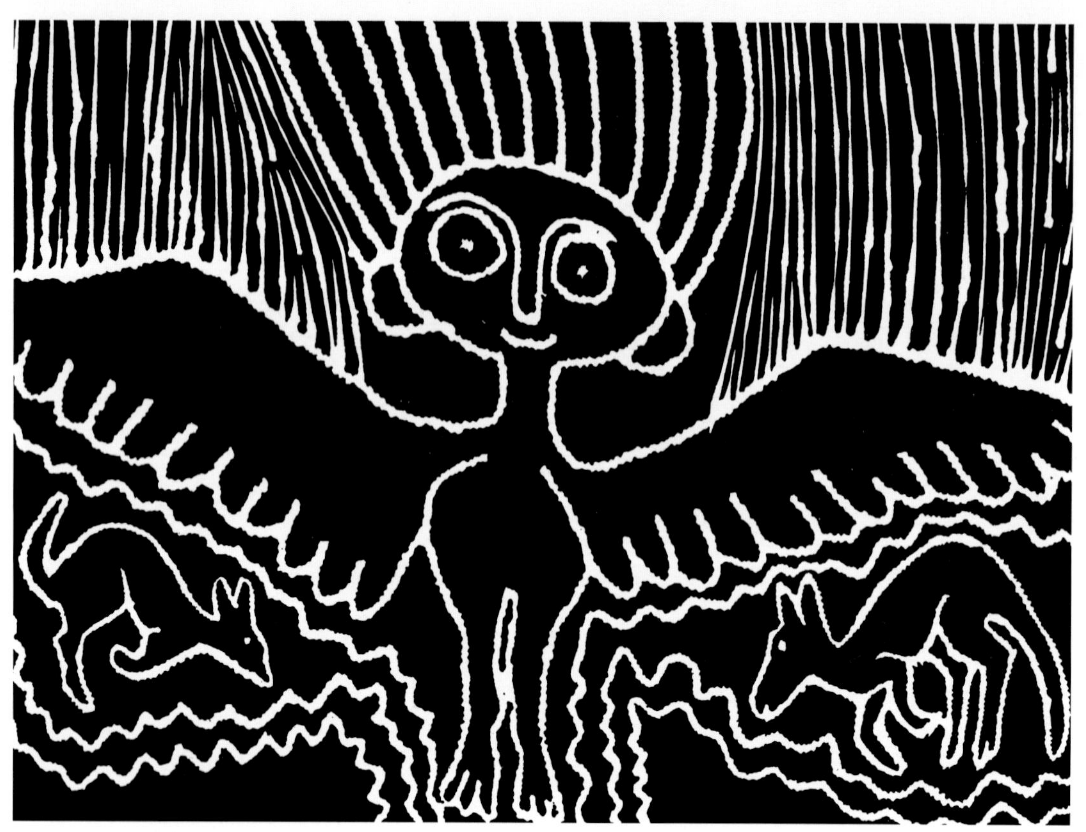

Mangkaja 1985
screenprint
33.6 x 45.5 cm
Edition: 54/95

Mangkaja or *Wirringarri* is a white bird from the Dreamtime. He is like an owl, with black and white markings around his eyes. He travels at night. *Mangkaja* came from *Kiyili* way. Some people were frightened of this *Mangkaja*. They found him sitting down on a log. They tried to kill him, but he flew up very high, and where he landed there sprung up a waterhole, *Mankaja Kura*. Nearby this place is *Malajapi*, the campsite of the *Mala* spirit. *Mala* is the little bush kangaroo. The people come here to tell the spirit to send plenty of mala to the land.

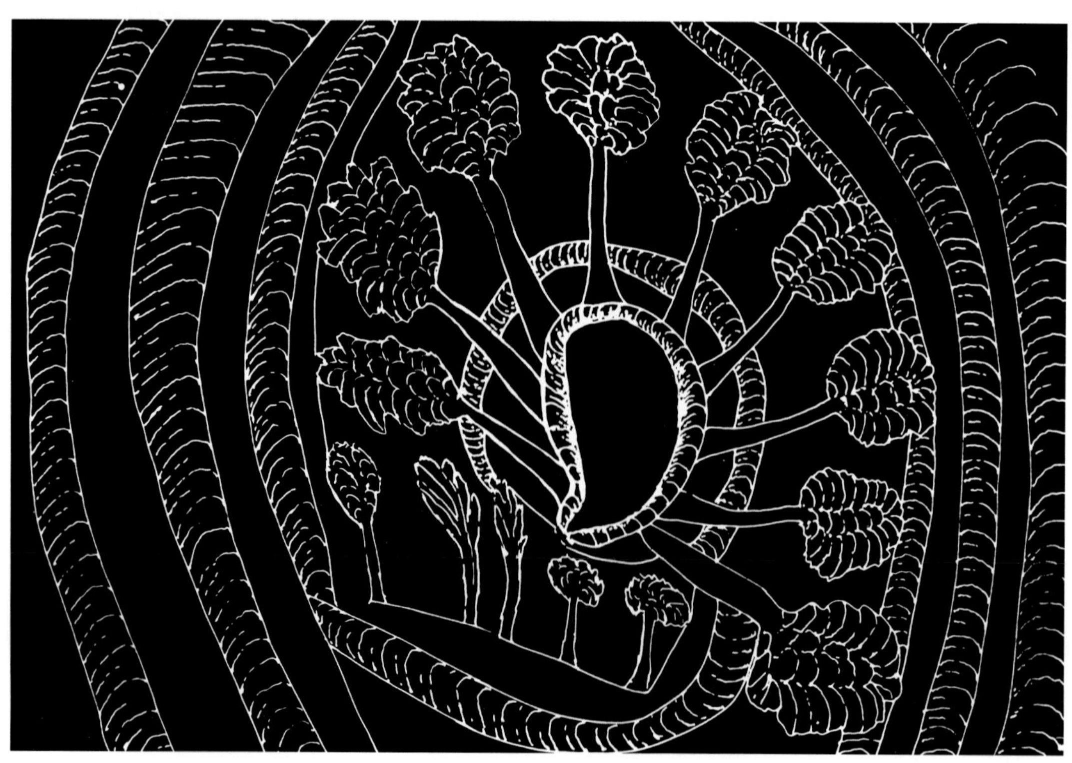

Parapara Karnparn and Wirrikari 1985
screenprint
30.2 x 44.6 cm
Edition: 24/80

Flat land between two sandhills on both sides. *Kurrkuminti* is the hollow in sandhill round the waterholes.

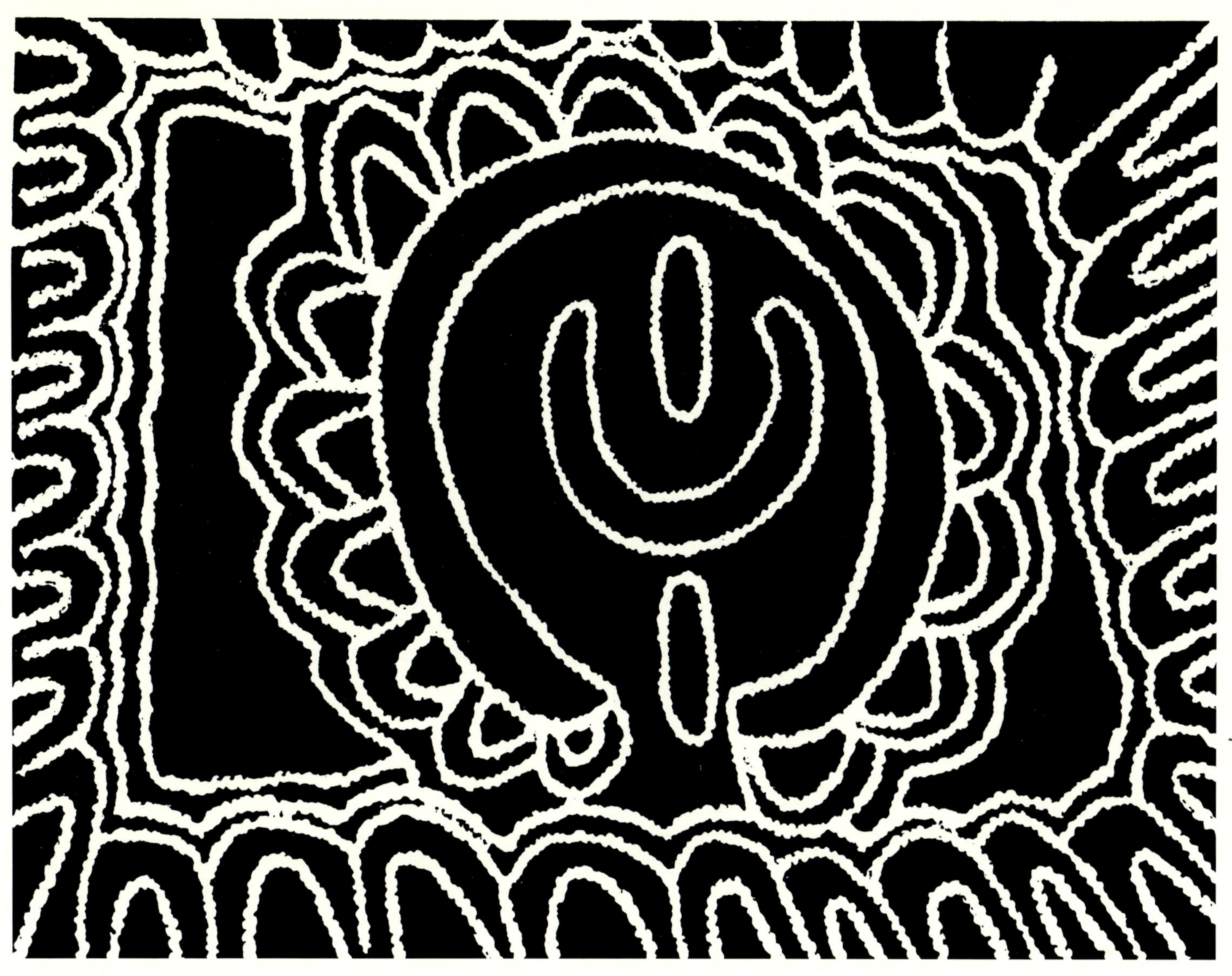

Payarr Rockhole 1985
screenprint
33.0 x 43.0 cm
Edition: 44/65

Grandfather and grandson been living in this place in Dreamtime. Old man sleeping by fire in rock shelter. Young man sleep outside – told 'this place for old men'. Young man cover himself with sand, build little wall to cover himself. They don't let him in. They punish him. When this old fella go to sleep, big rain comes in. Young fella wakes up. Grabs that firestick from there, and puts him in another place, hides it under a rock hole. Comes back and finds old man still asleep. He get all the food and take it and get the firestick from the other rock hole. Old man got up and there was nothing – no fire. Looking around and calling out Bu Bu – sound like big bird – he answers. He tracked him right up to *Kulijirri,* a little water hole, nearest one. He got a big sandhill. He follows him up to big sandhill. Young man cooking kangaroo, with two dogs. They argue about the fire. The two dogs they grab the old man, they fight him. They kill him right there. He turns into two rocks. He roll down the hill to waterhole named *Kulkurr* far away.

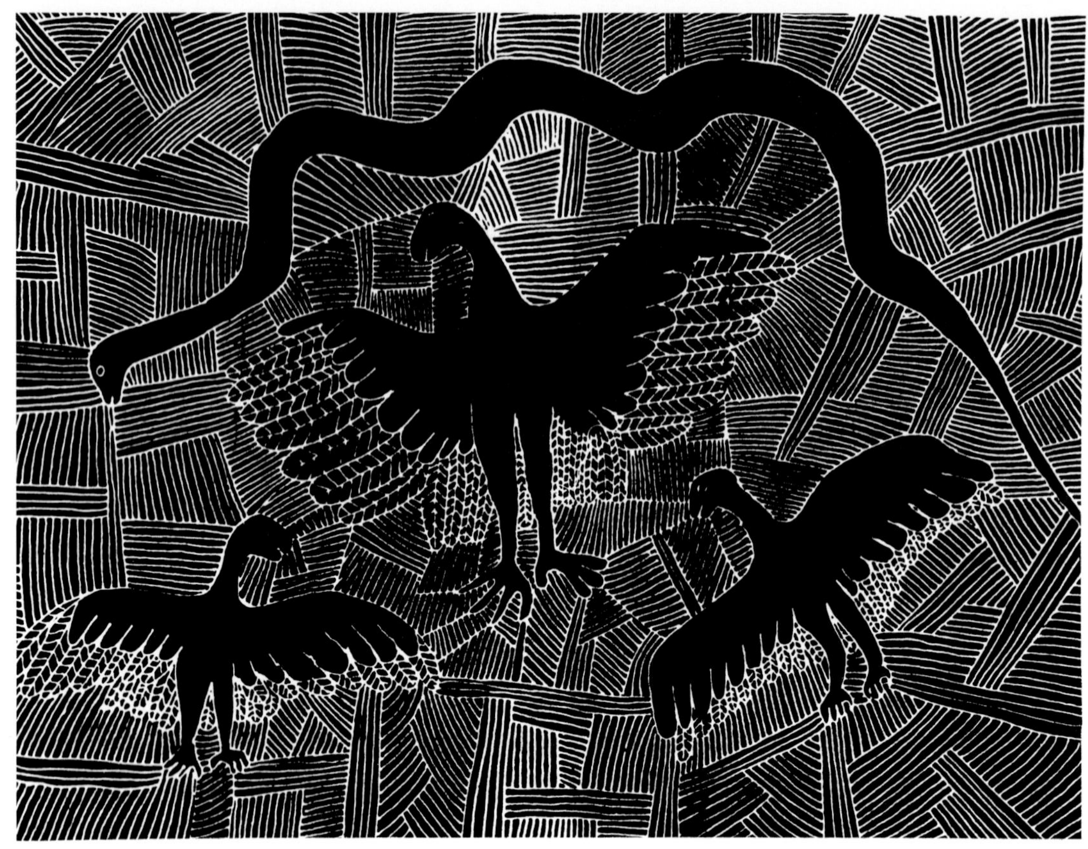

**Kirrikirri –
Chickenhawk** 1985
screenprint
31.0 x 40.6 cm
Edition: 63/80

Sometimes they kill a
snake when they are
landing. They kill a big
one or a small one.

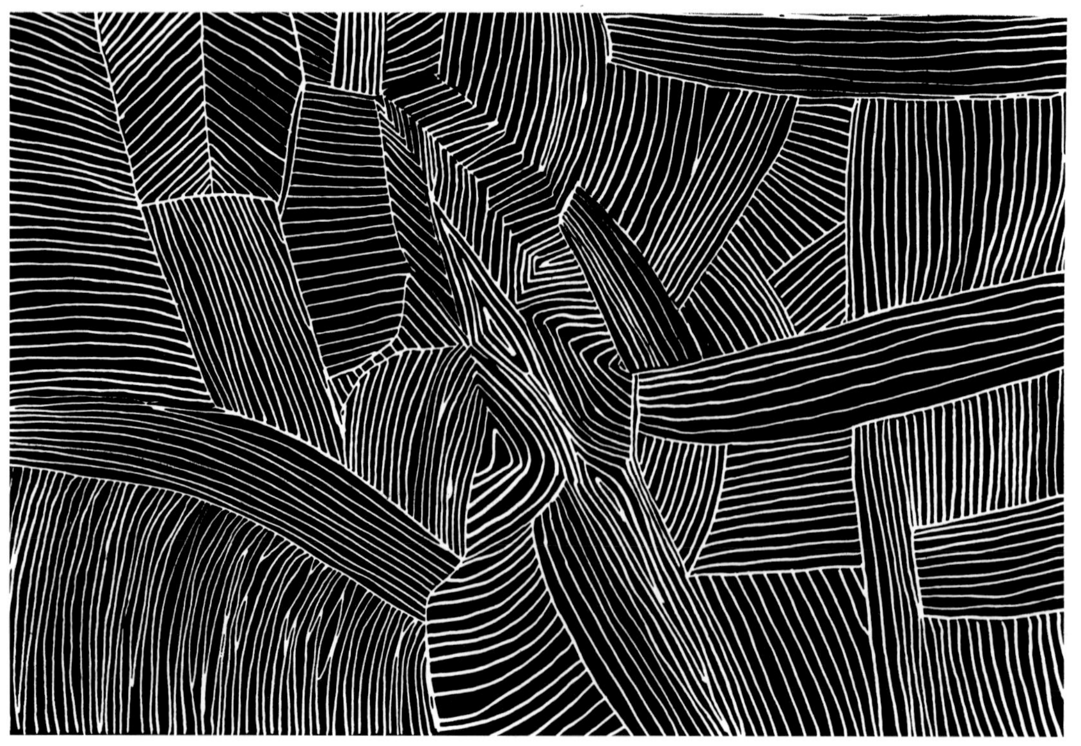

Jilji Kurrmalya 1985
screenprint
33.5 x 49.6 cm
Edition: 3/40

Sandhills – *Kurrkuminti-
Kurrkuminti* – hollow
surrounded by sandhills.
People used to walk
around that area looking
for food.

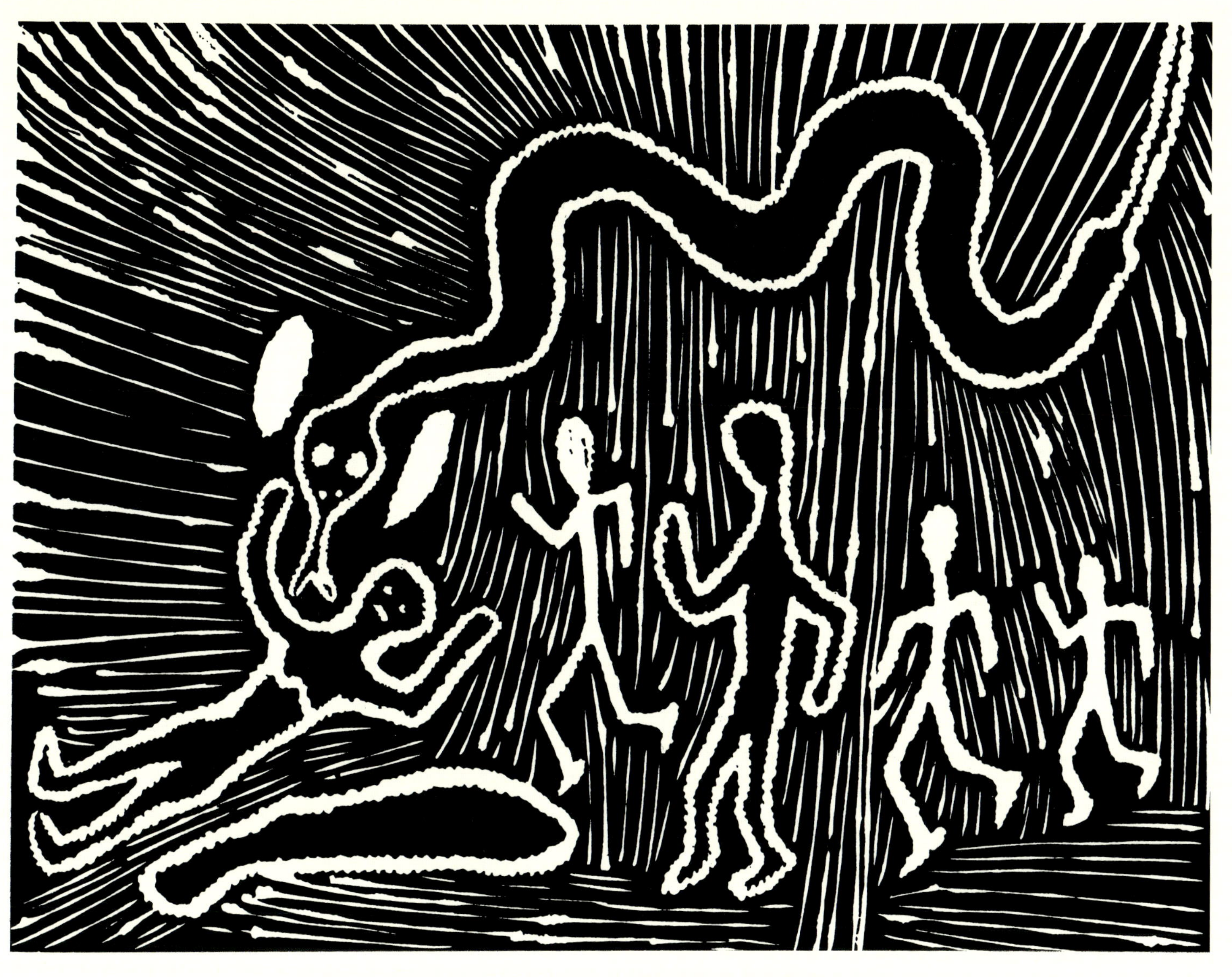

Ngalyawiltirr 1985
screenprint
33.3 x 43.0 cm
Edition: 42/75

Woman went hunting for *Milkarra*. Leave four children
at that place. She went hunting to *Ngalyawiltirr*, she get
bitten by snake, death adder. She put her hand in kangaroo
hole and get bitten by snake. Children follow her track all
the way from *Milkarra*. They find her dead.

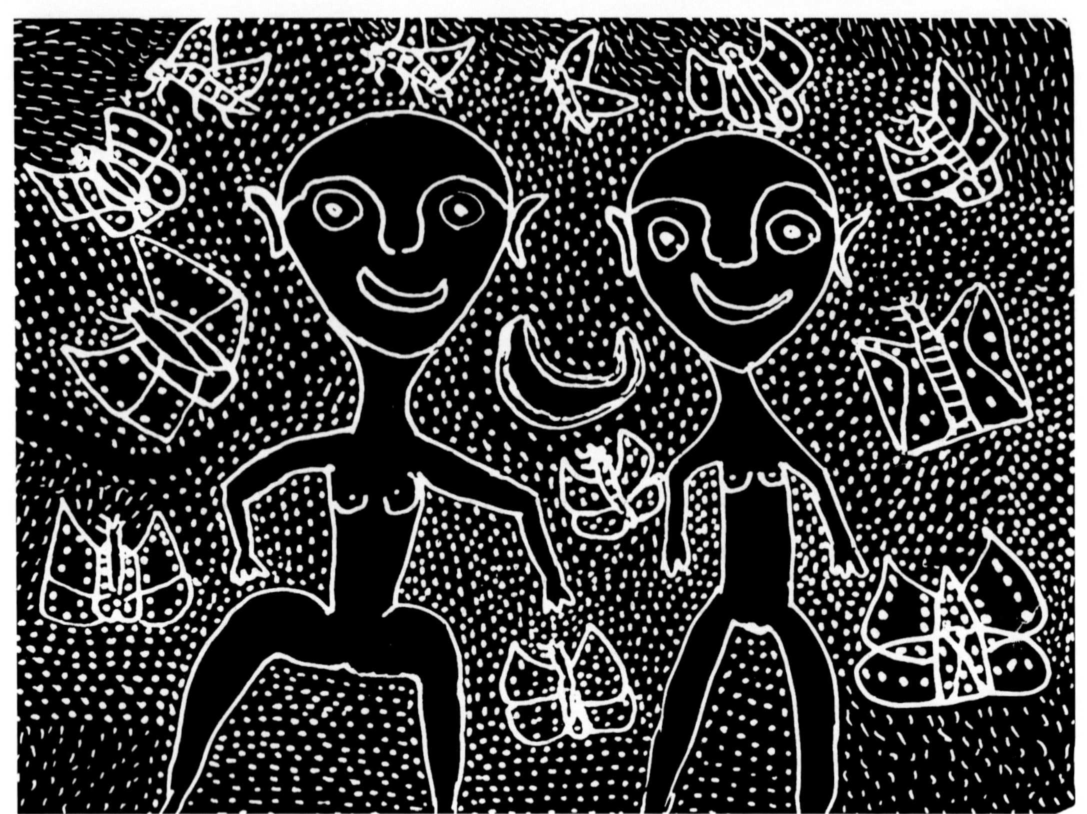

Two Little Girls 1987
screenprint
27.5 x 38.0 cm
Edition: 15/95

One mother had two baby girls, in one waterhole. Two girls find butterfly flying towards them. They try to grab them. They miss them. They chase them all the way. They come up to a big mob of women, who pick up the two girls. The mother come back and find them. She follow their tracks and come to the women and asked for her two girls, but they wouldn't give her back her two babies.

Mangajarra Pinya Martanani Ngamajirlu Karlkali Ngapanga Karlkawurtula.

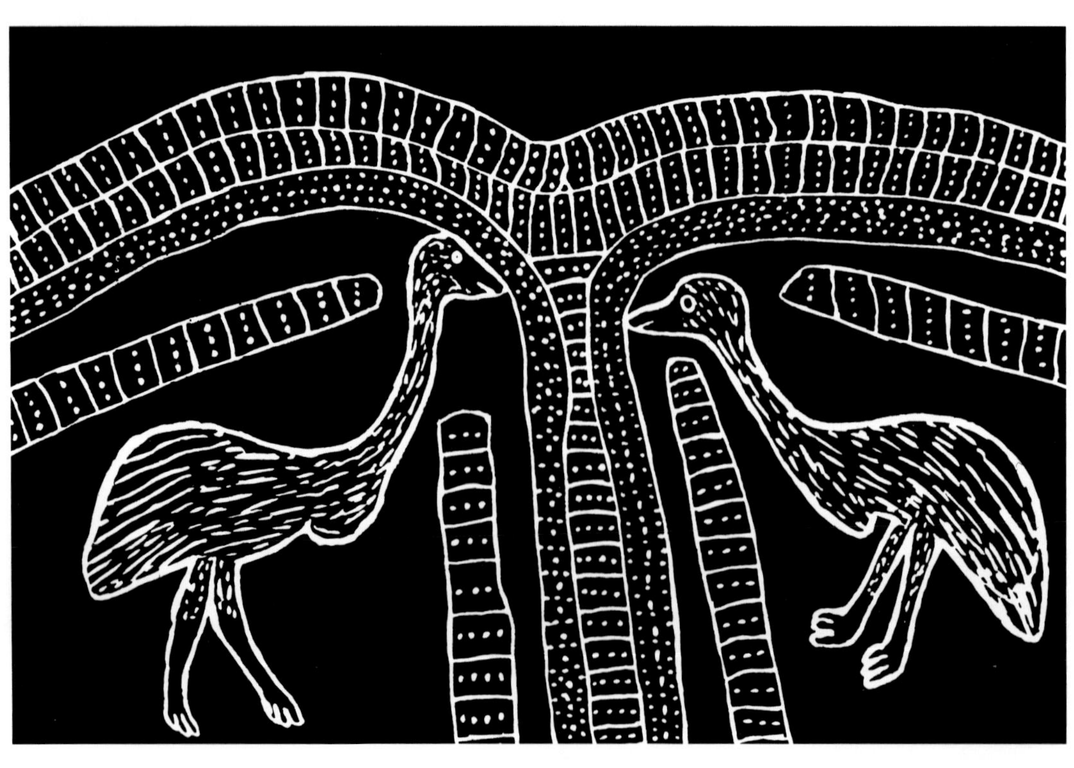

Karnanganyja – Two Emus 1988
screenprint
33.5 x 49.5 cm
Edition: 19/95

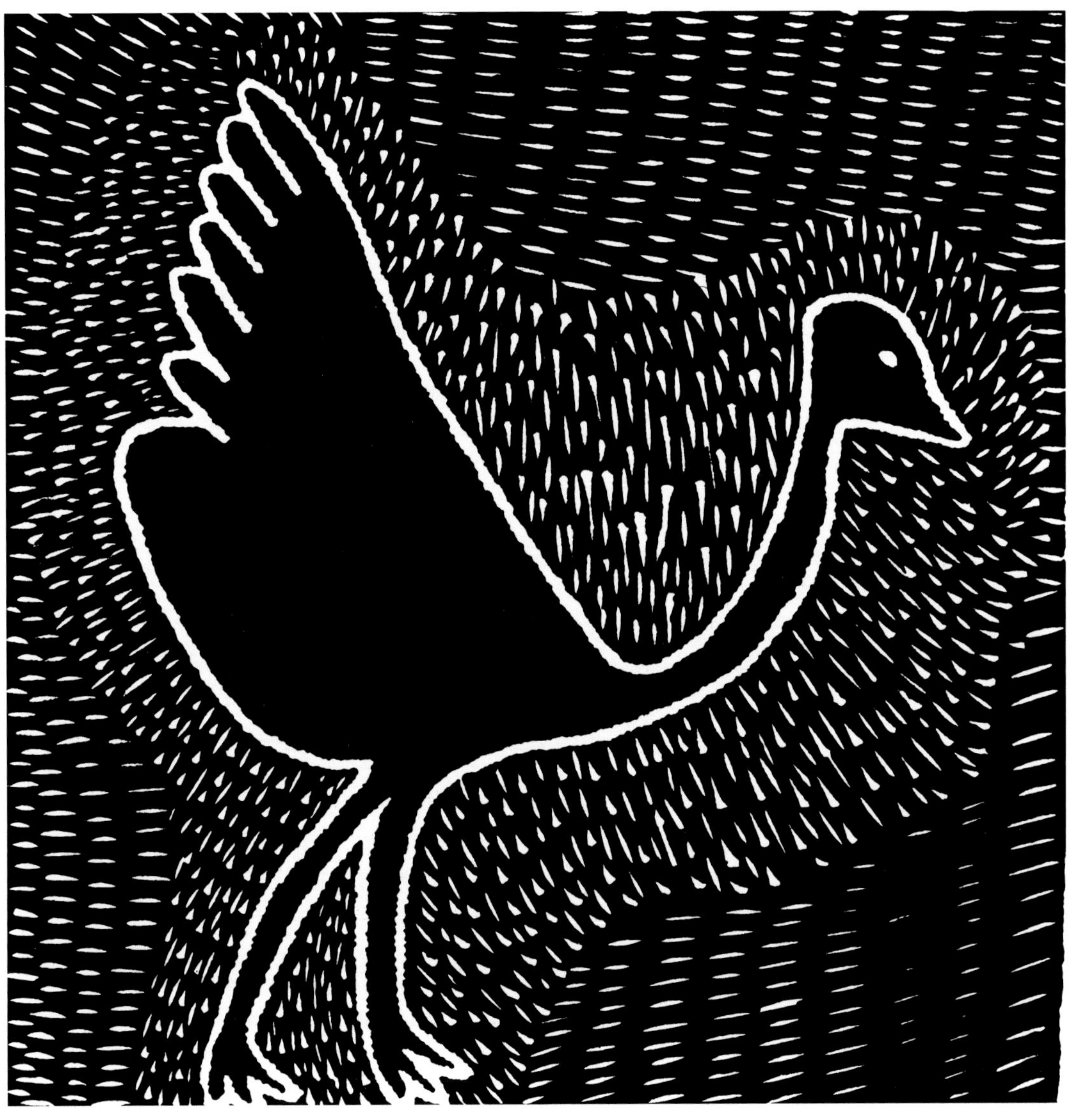

Pirnini Country I 1987
screenprint
32.5 x 31.8 cm
Edition: 20/75

A billabong story, water right round and a swan.

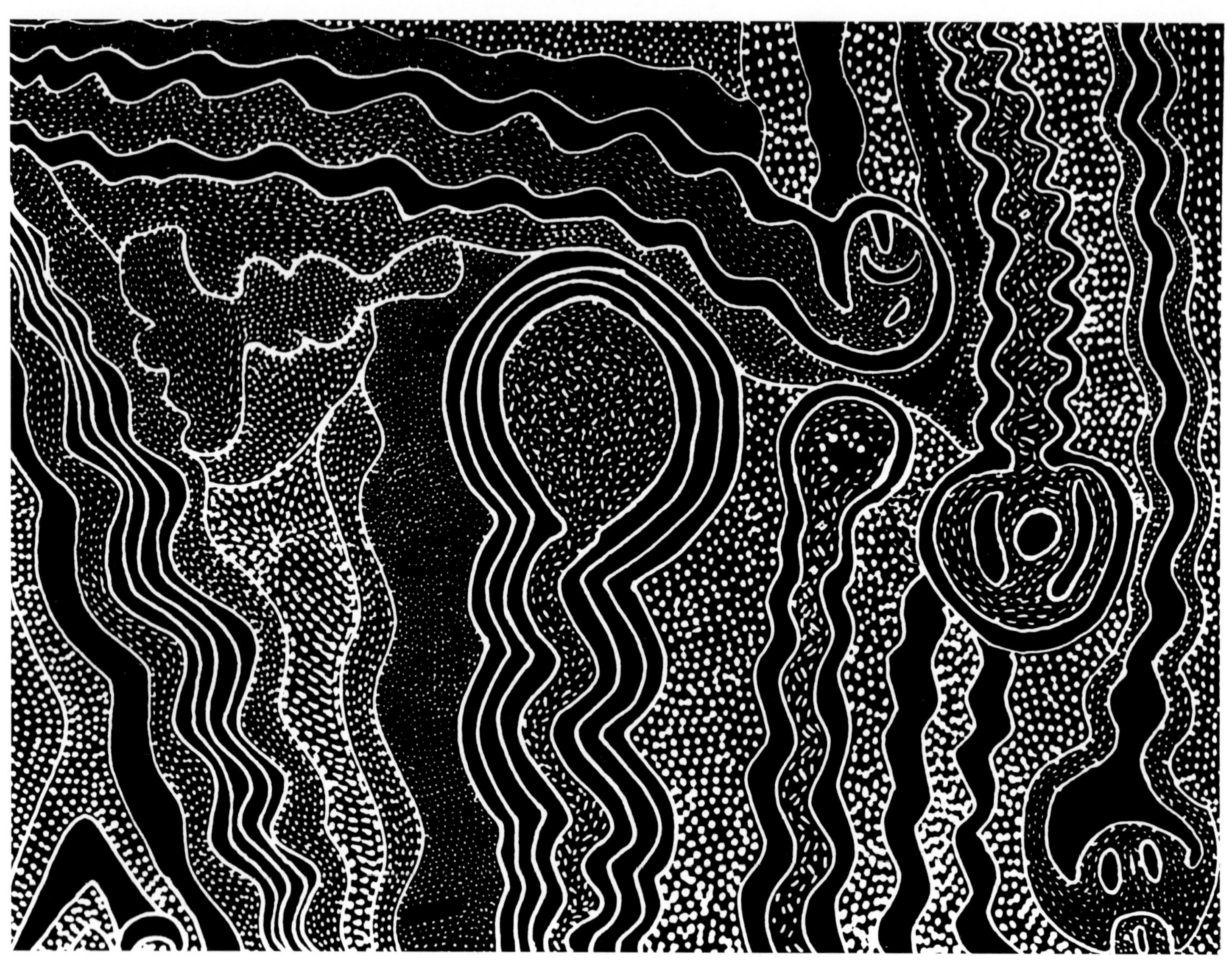

Woman Carrying her Two Boys 1988
screenprint
34.0 x 35.3 cm
Edition: 19/95

Sandhill Country 1988
screenprint
33.3 x 45.0 cm
Edition: 19/95

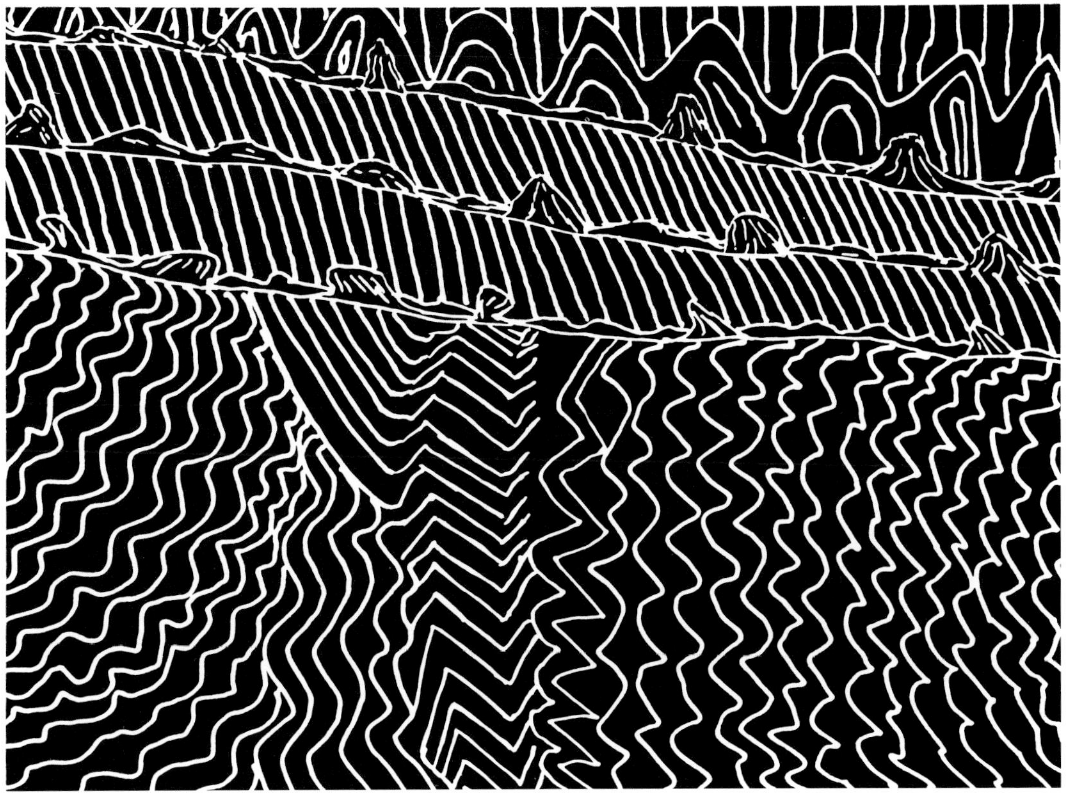

Jilji and Jimu 1988
screenprint
34.0 x 44.8 cm
Edition: 19/95

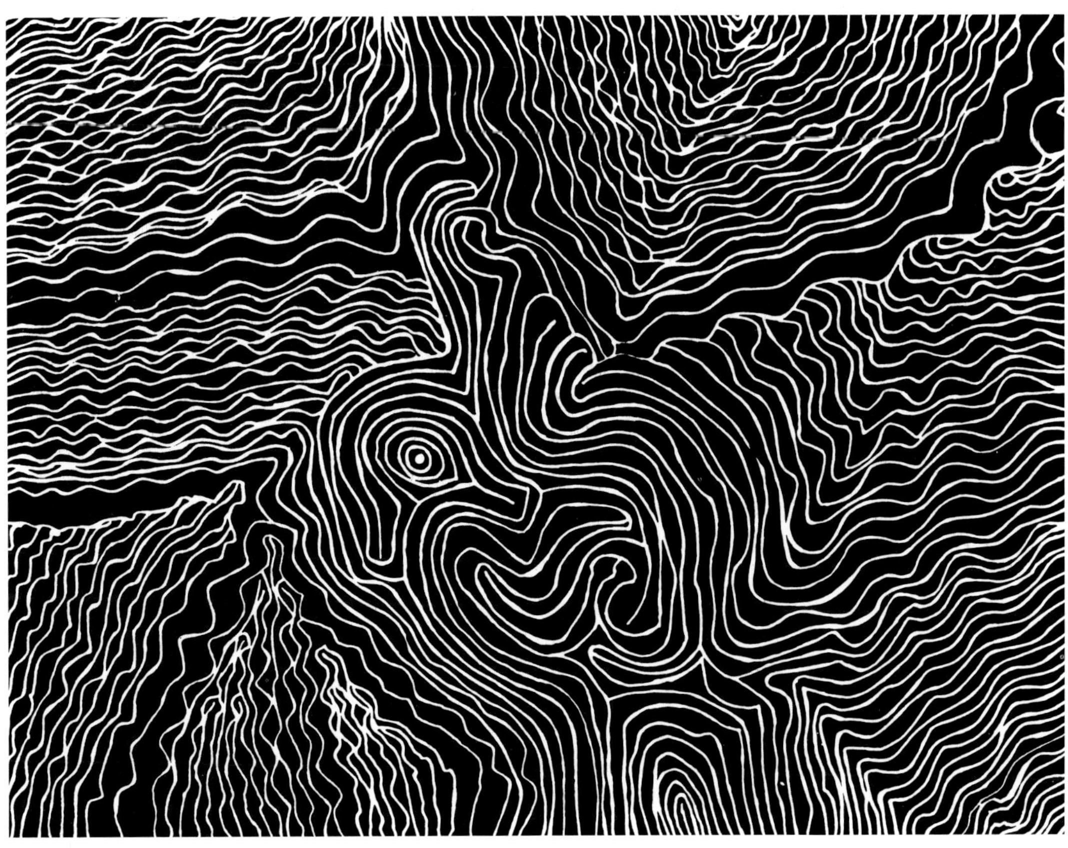

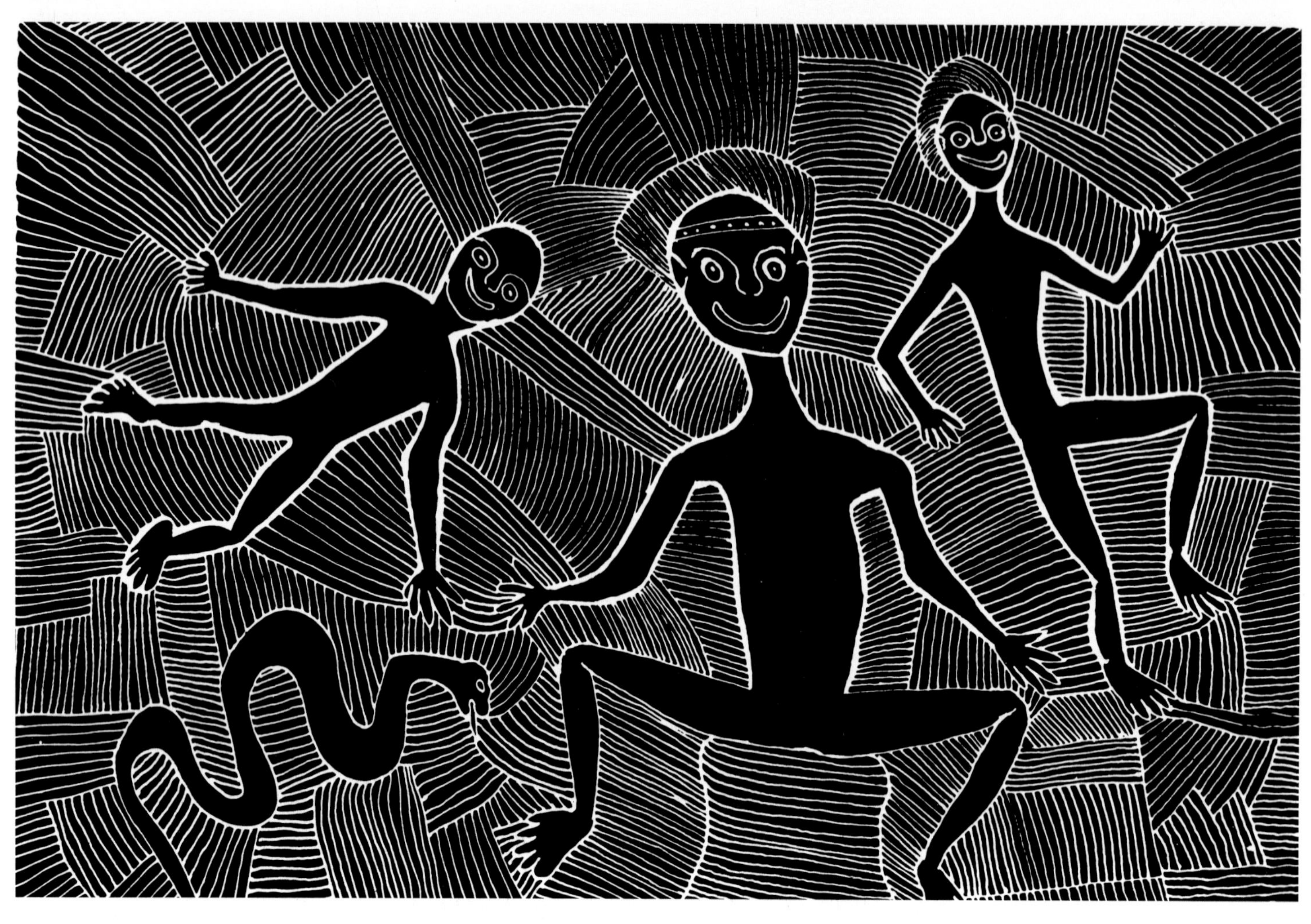

A Man and His Wife and Her Small Children 1988
screenprint
33.8 x 50.5 cm
Edition: 20/95

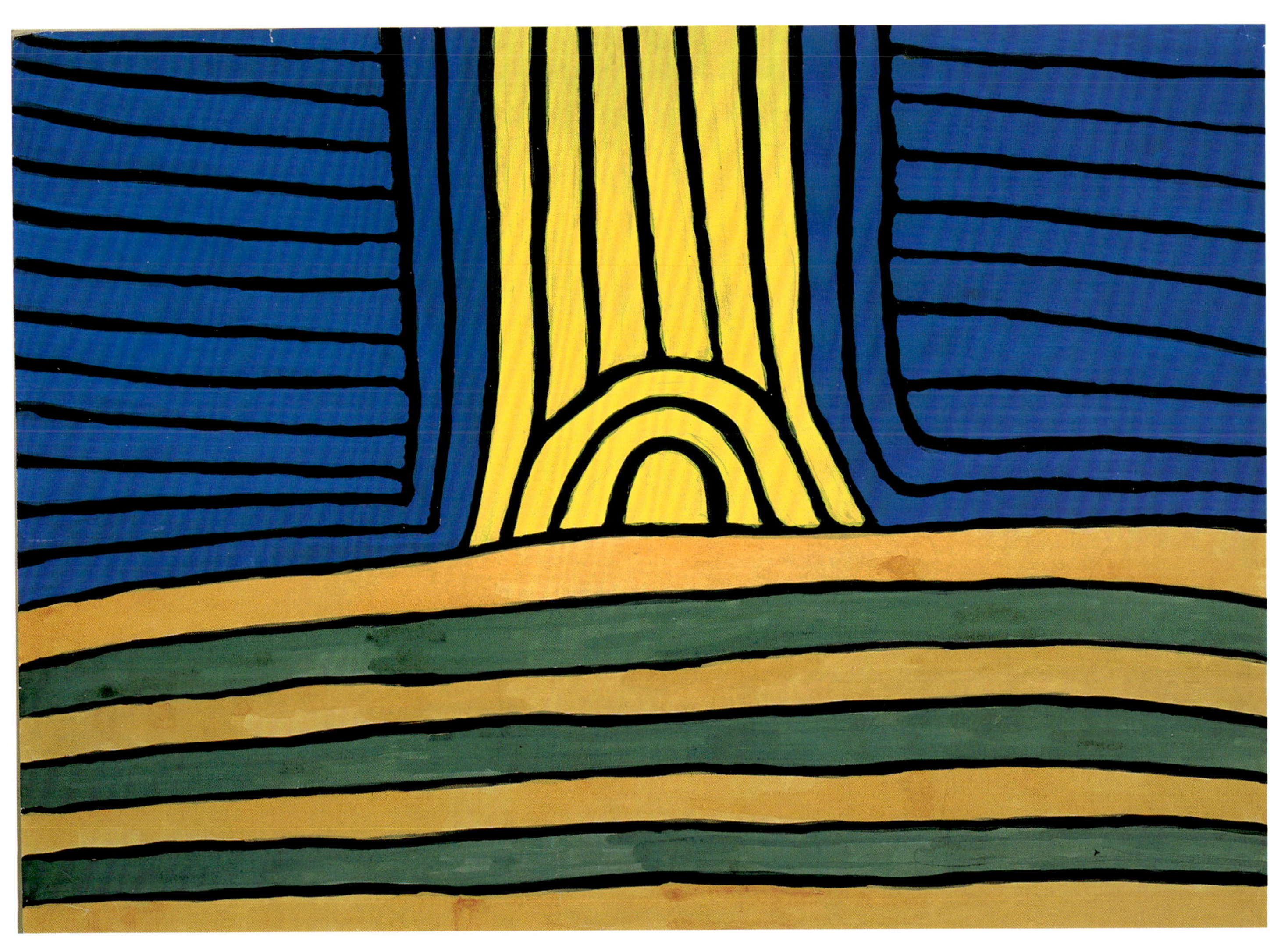

Rakaralla–Koonbunda 1982/83
Early morning sunlight – sunrise
acrylic paint on paper
59.5 x 84.5 cm
Desert Designs Collection

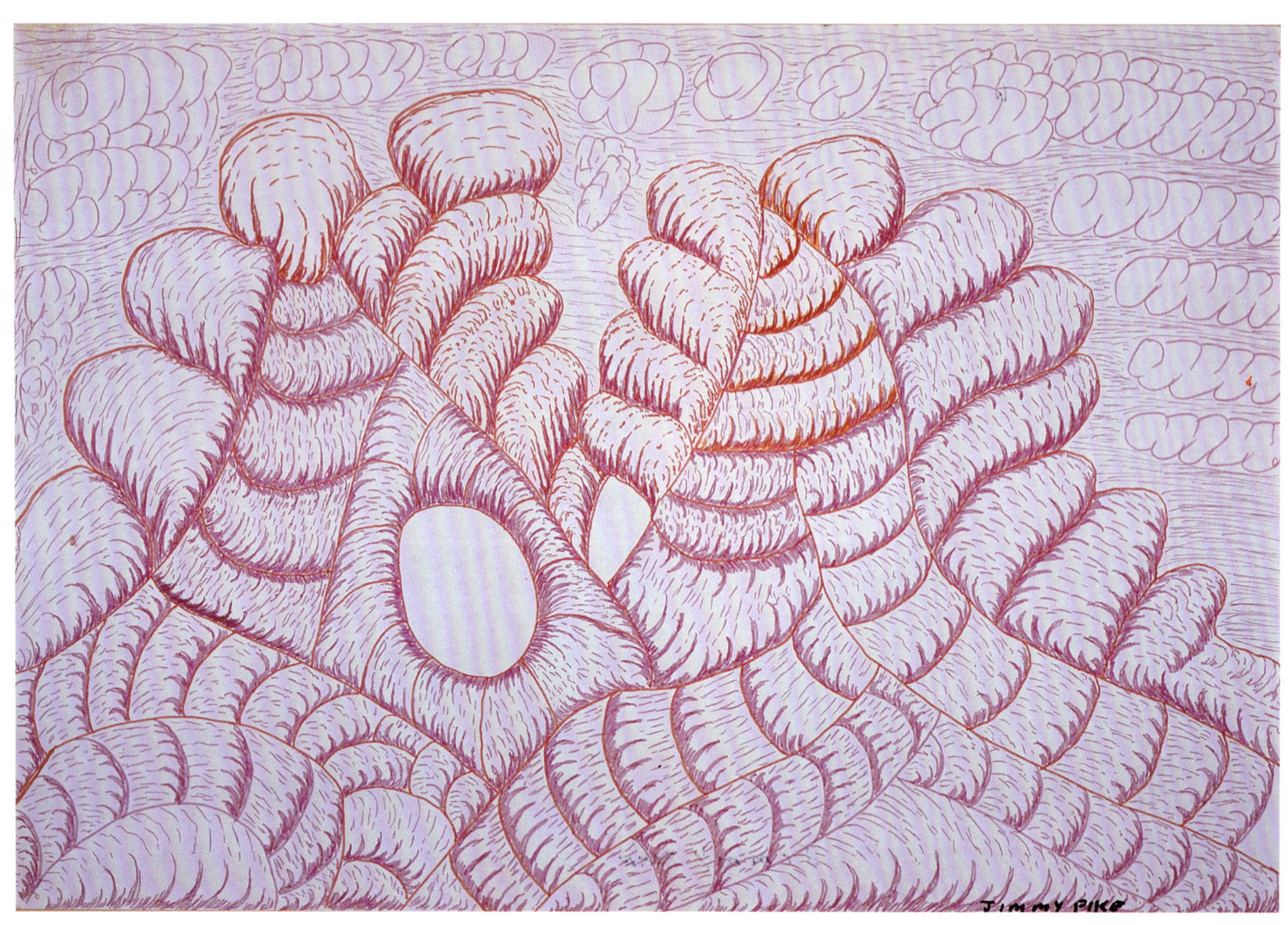

Rocky landscape 1987 / 8
Textacolour pen on paper
37.2 x 55.5 cm
Desert Designs Collection

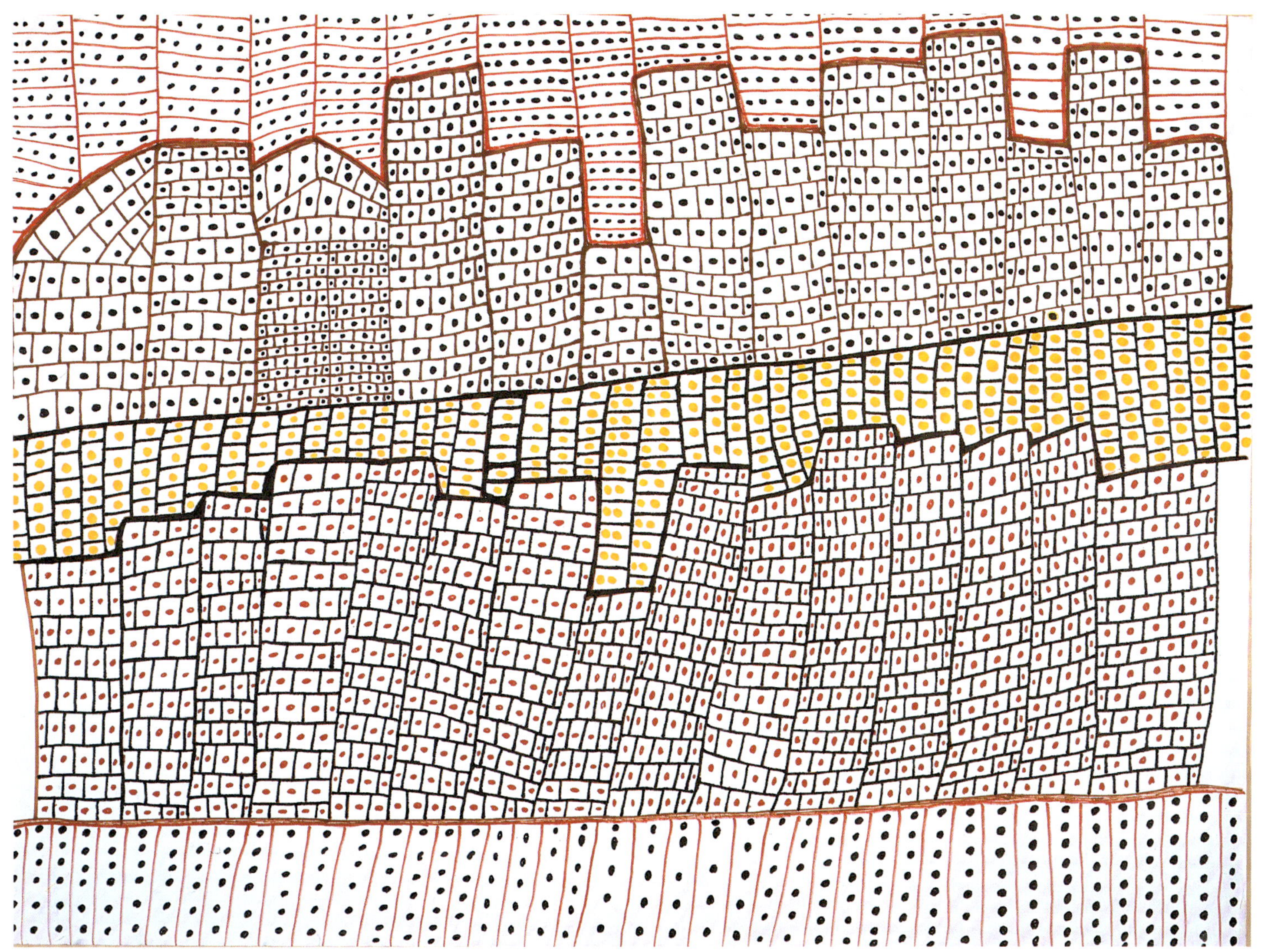

Cityscape 1981/82
Textacolour pen on paper
55.5 x 75.7 cm
Desert Designs Collection

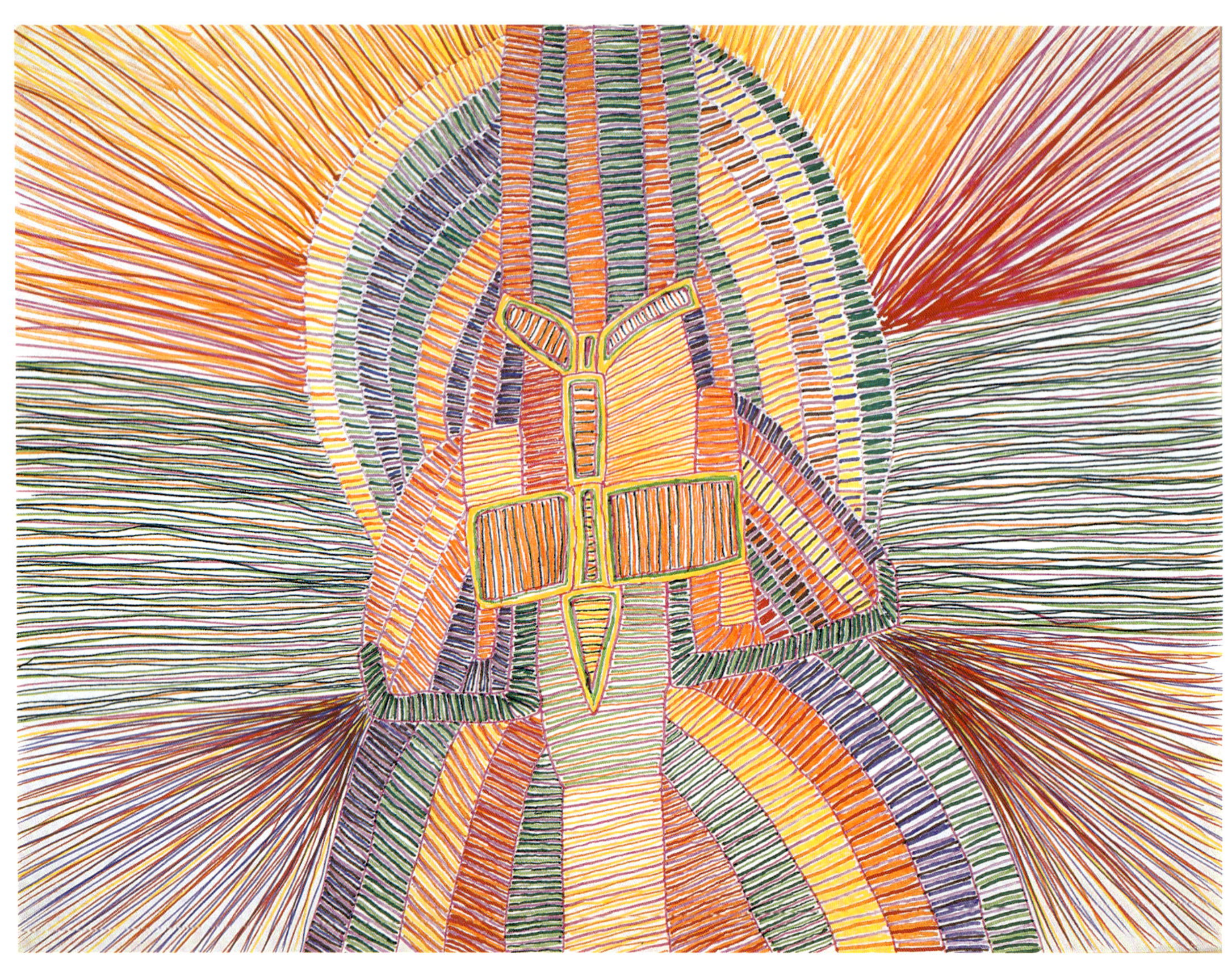

Yarriplan – Aeroplane c.1983
Textacolour pen on paper
38.0 x 51.0 cm
Desert Designs Collection

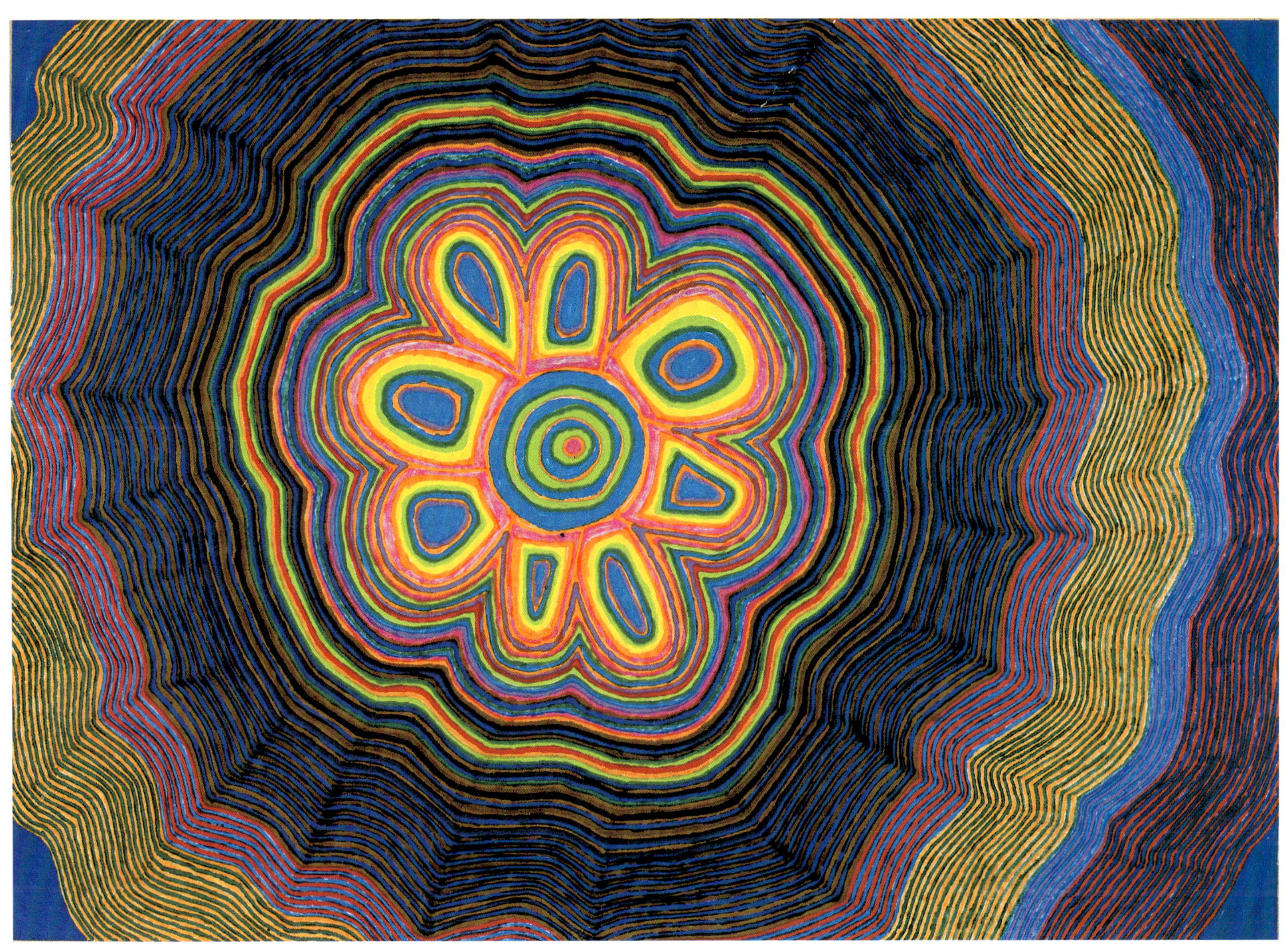

Jila – Waterhole c.1983
Textacolour pen on paper
41.7 x 59.0 cm
Desert Designs Collection

Dreamtime man left food buried around *jila*.
Green stones like emu eggs [were left] where food was
buried. The people know that there is food at this place.

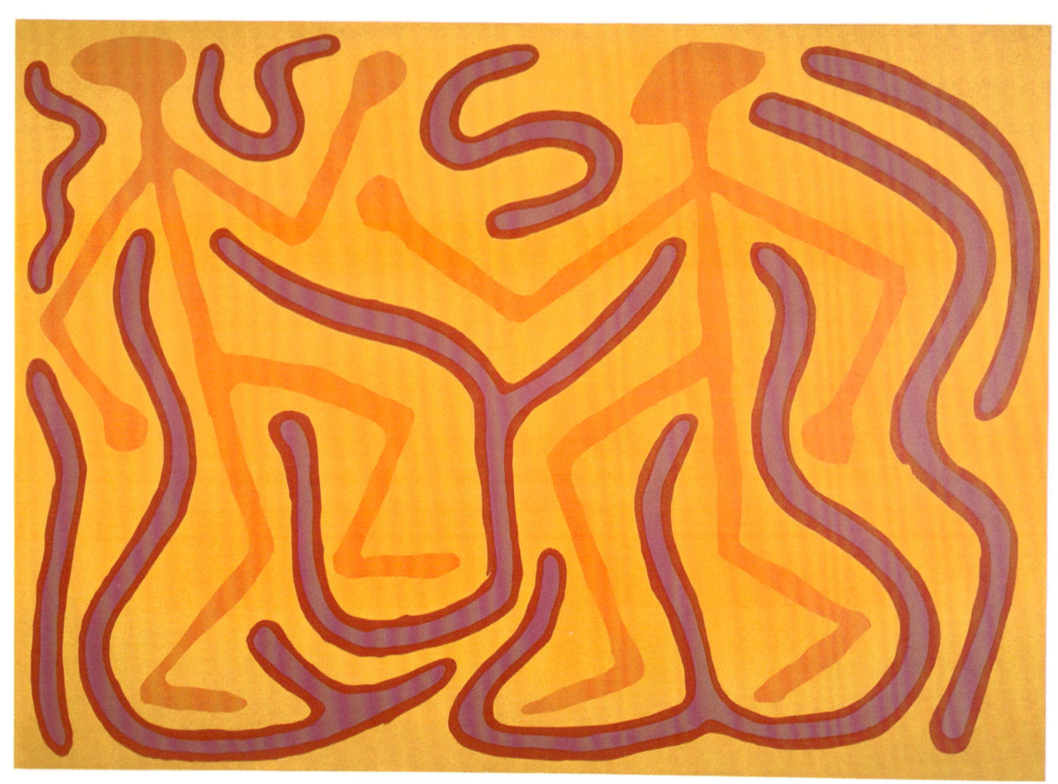

**Mangarakarra/
Jukurrani/
Ngarangkarni** 1985
colour screen print
59.5 x 84.6 cm
Edition: 31/35

The three names in the title
are alternatives for the
same Dreamtime being.

Two men in a windbreak,
like a cave. They are two
cousin brothers, lying
down. They been travelling
from the north. The
Dreamtime start first,
put everything down.
People been follow.

*Jukarrani Parla
Jukurrjukurrpinya*

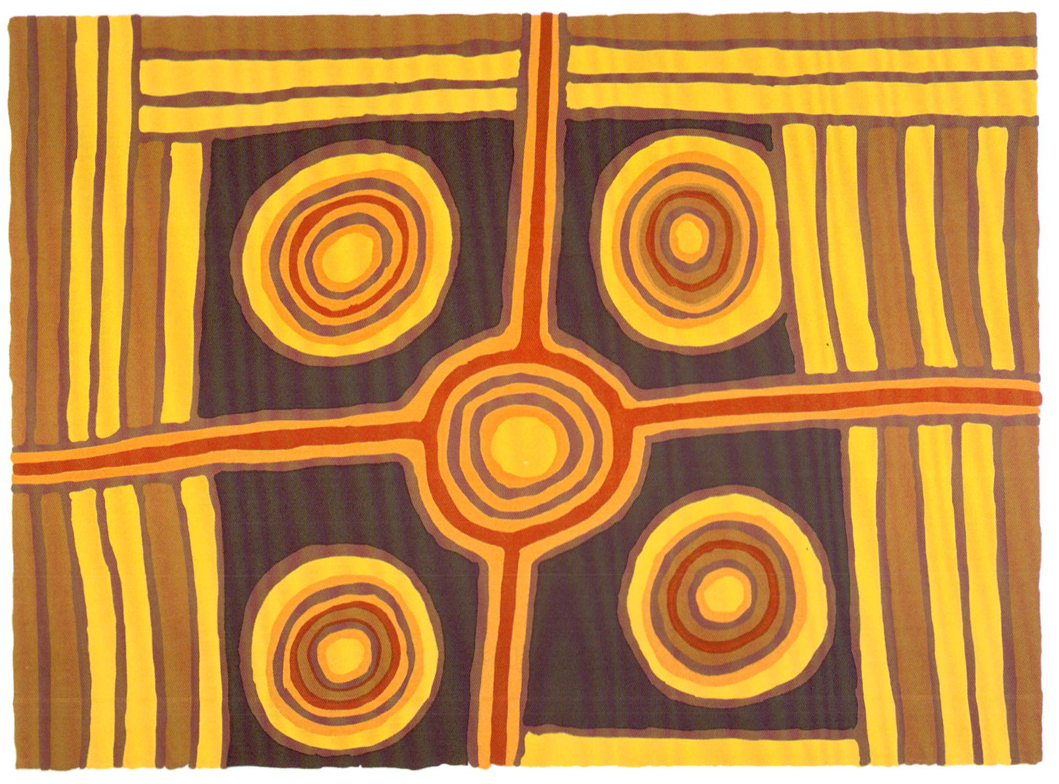

Jumangkarni 1985
colour screen print
59.8 x 84.5 cm
Edition: 3/25

Dreamtime people went
north and east, big mob
people, thousands. They
cross one another. Big mob
from south, they went
north, and another mob
went north-east.
They never came back.

Larripuka 1986
colour screen print
40.7 x 50.6 cm
Edition: 53/80

Country. People been
walking past Dreamtime.
Some disappeared right
there. This is a pattern of
the sandhills. People use
that for carving, right up to
today. This law is passed
from grandfather to father
to son.

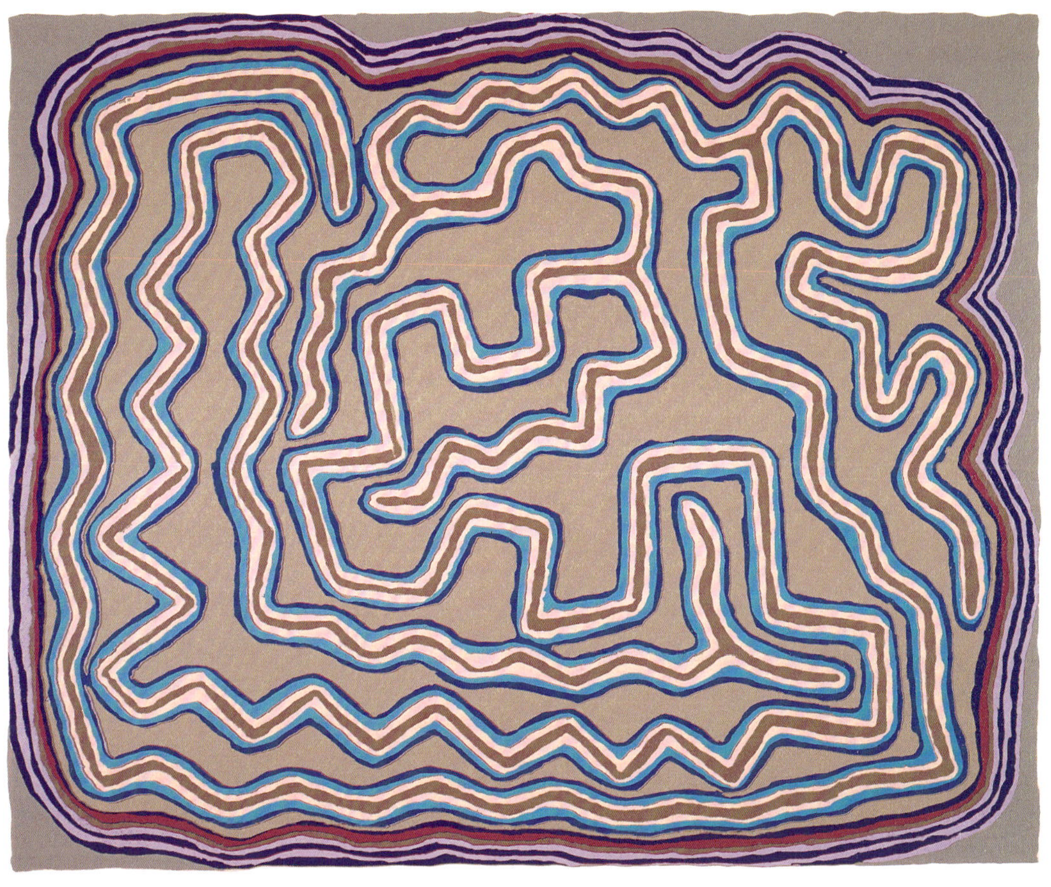

Jilji Kulku Nganpayi
1985
colour screen print
37.8 x 50.5 cm
Edition: 28/35

The story of *Muutulya*.
He been walking in the
bush looking for water.
He find all *punyanangu*.
Punyanangu is like a well.
You can find it anywhere,
digging. Soft sand fall on
top of him, and kill him.
People can still use that
water today. Make a hole
anywhere and find water.

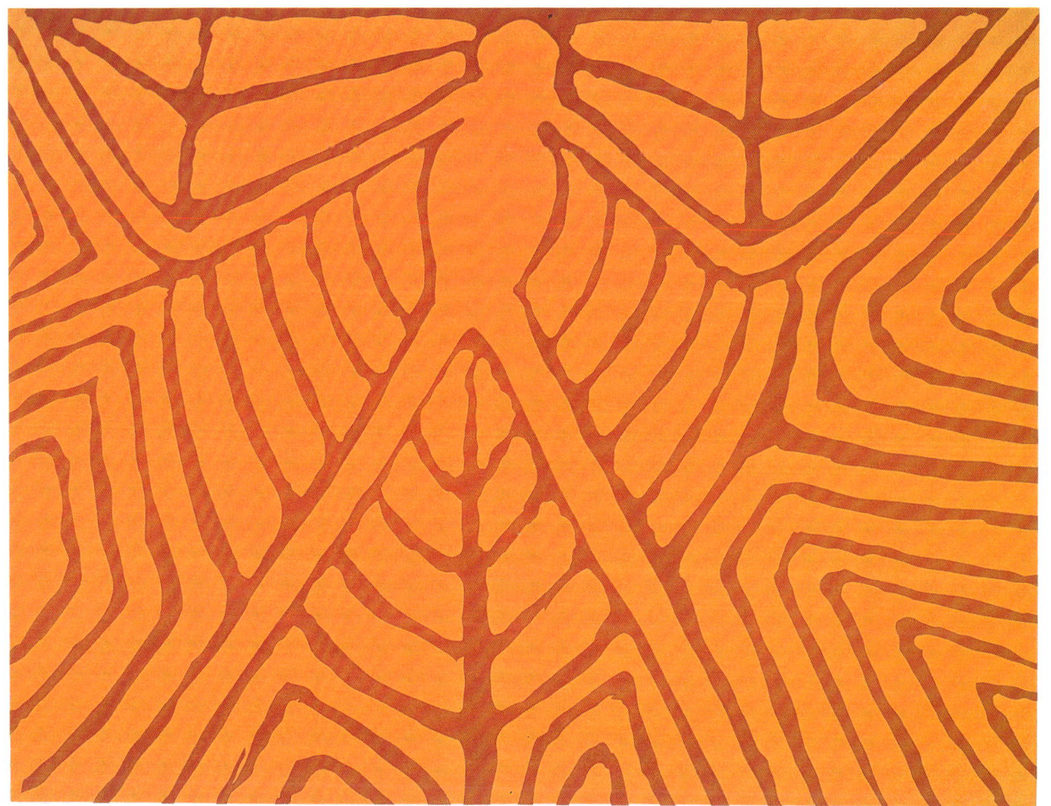

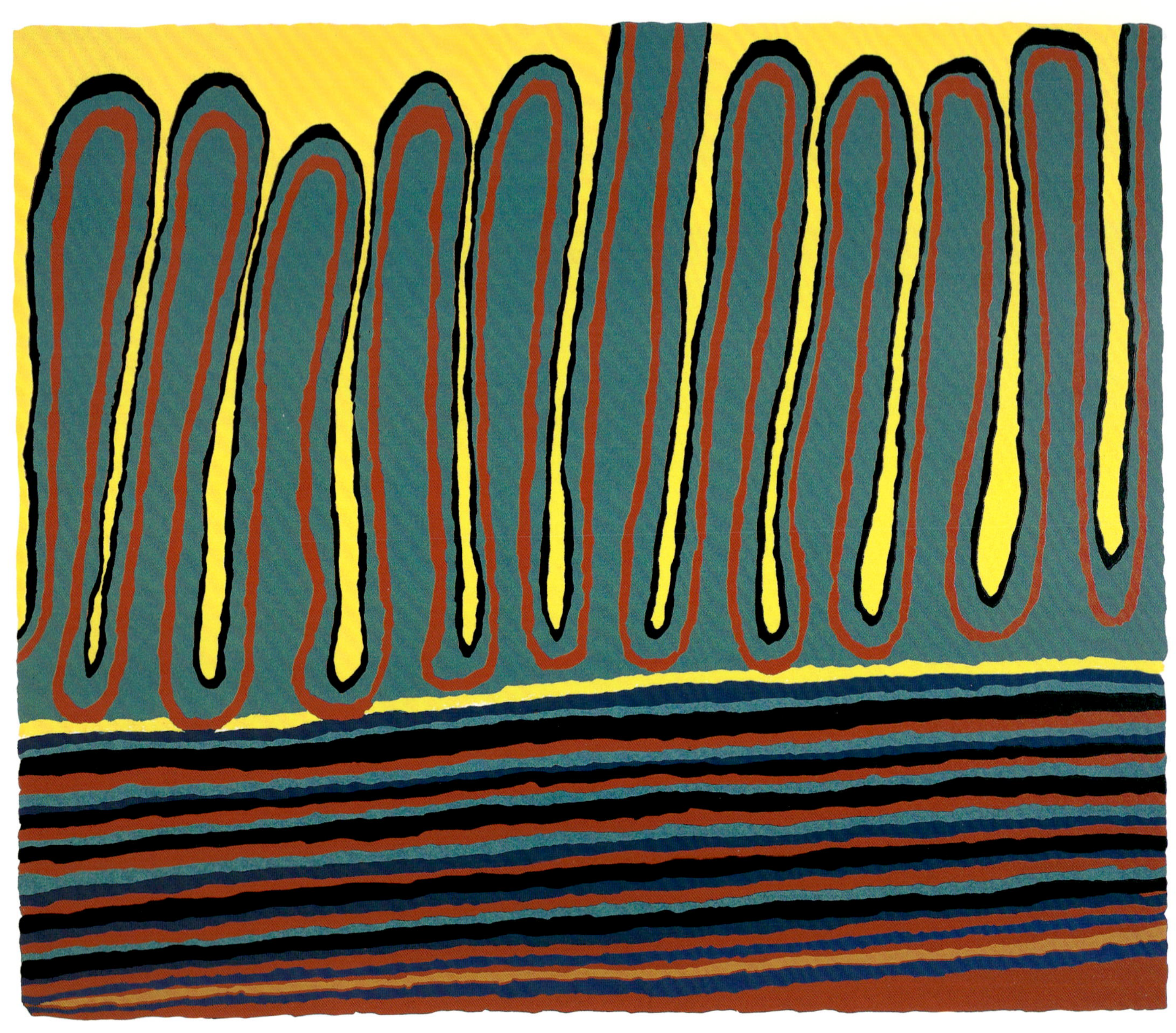

Jilji, Yuka, Partiri 1986
Sandhills, Grass and Flowers.
colour screen print
50.8 x 60.7 cm
Edition: 9/65

The black lines are *waruwaru* or burnt grass, might be burnt
last year, where green grows afterwards. The red and green
above are more grass and red ground, stony, called *pilpili*.

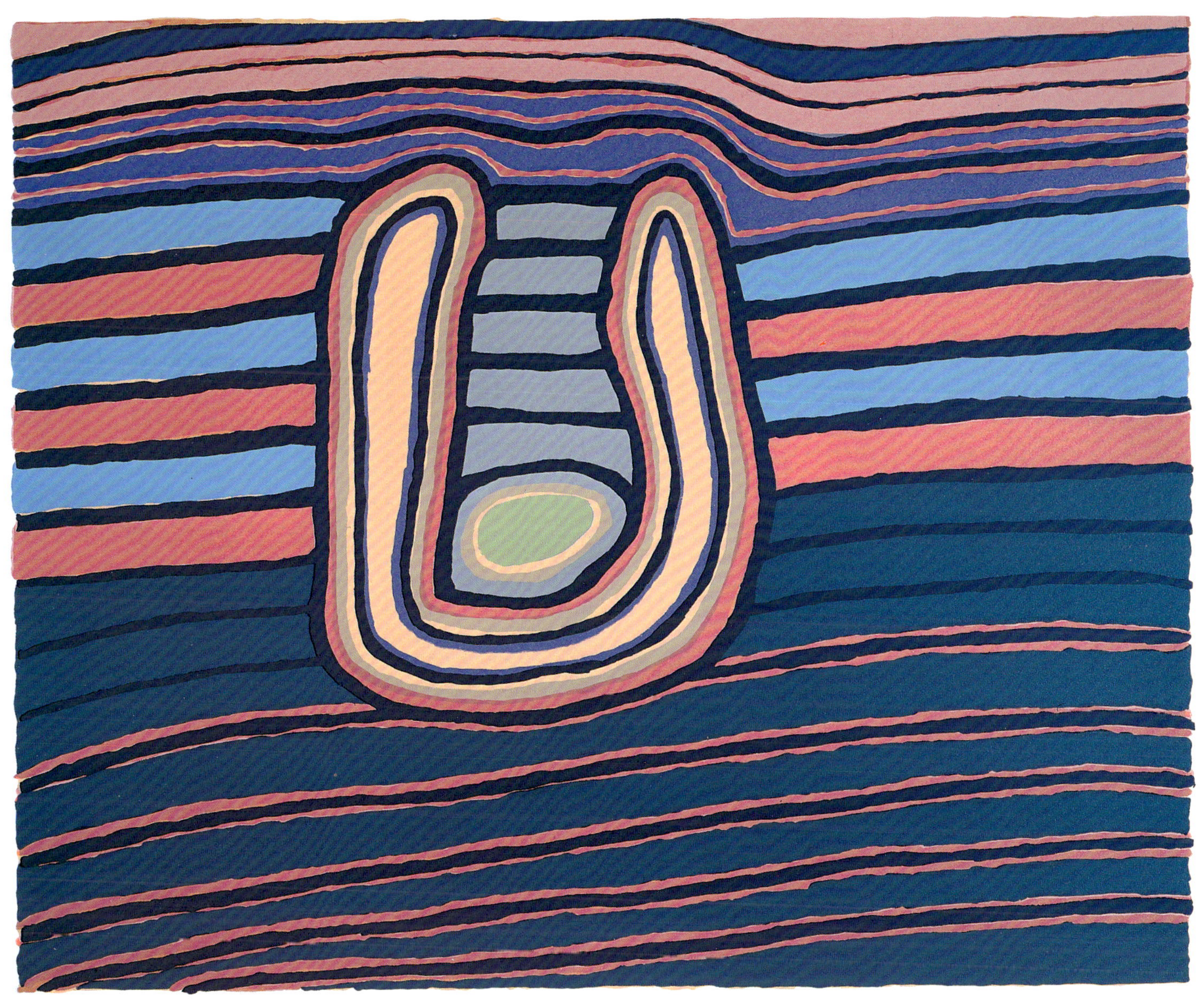

Two Men at a Waterhole 1986
colour screen print
40.6 x 50.0 cm
Edition: 7/60

Two men were sitting each side of a waterhole. This waterhole is *Tingki*. The two men are *Pitingaji* and *Wurta*; they
are wild with one another. They are having an argument
about the land. They are from different places and they
have story problems. They turned into two rocks by this
waterhole.

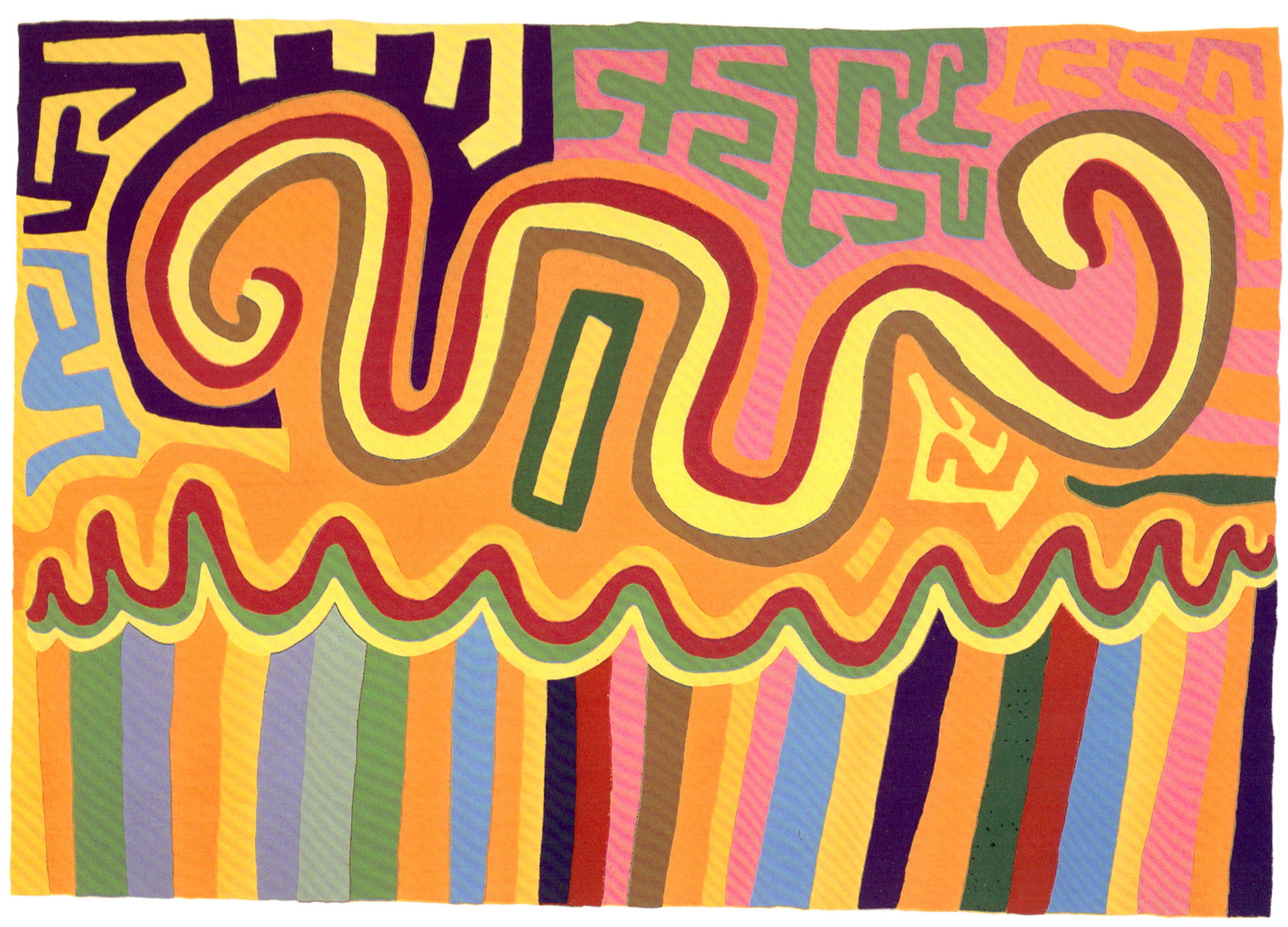

Body Painting – Purnara 1987
colour screen print
38.3 x 56.1 cm
Edition: 25/60

Used in law by people from that desert country.
Jiljis [sandhills] in the foreground.

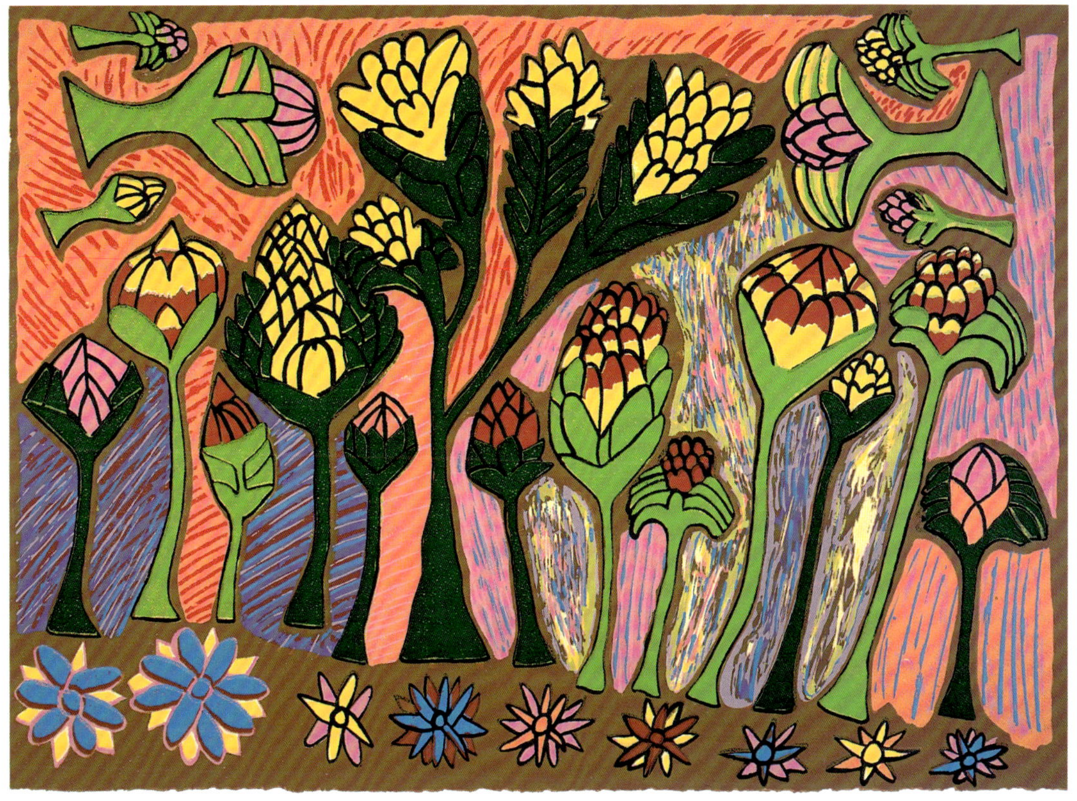

**Desert Flowers –
Partiri** 1986
colour screen print
42.5 x 59.5 cm
Edition: 52/65

After rain, green grass and
flowers come up, turn all
colours. In the bush, not
just near waterhole.

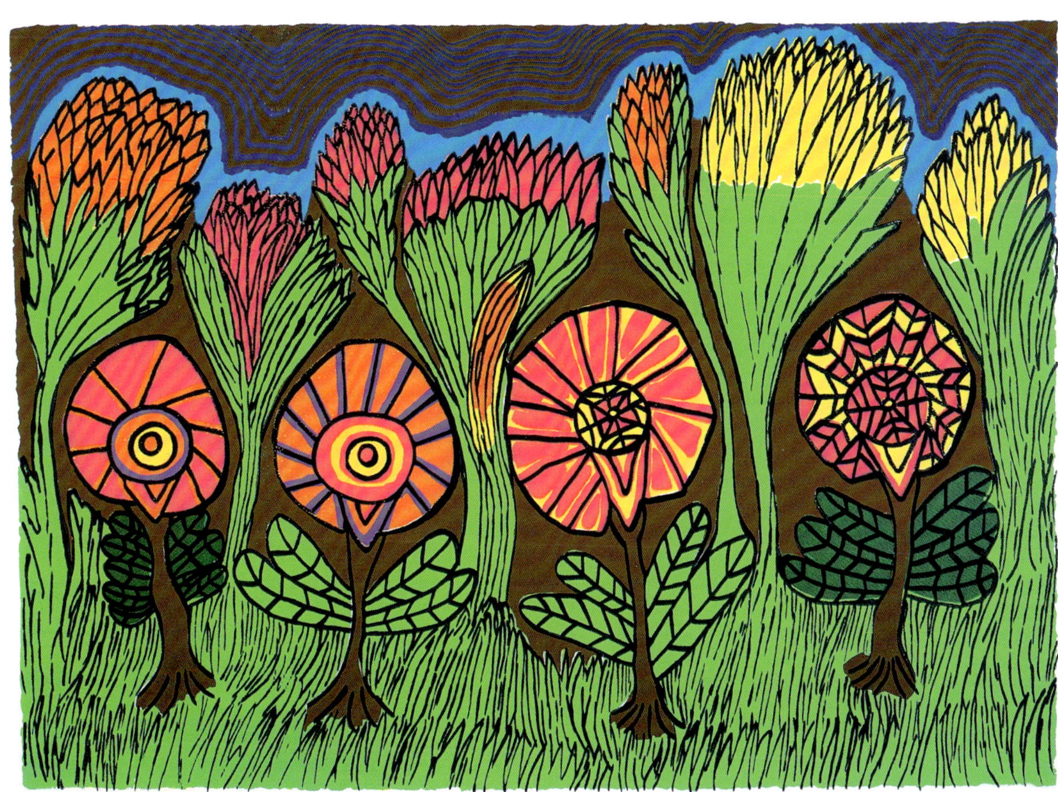

Flowers – Partiri 1987
colour screen print
41.8 x 58.5 cm
Edition: 27/55

Green grass time, after
rain, when everything
grows.

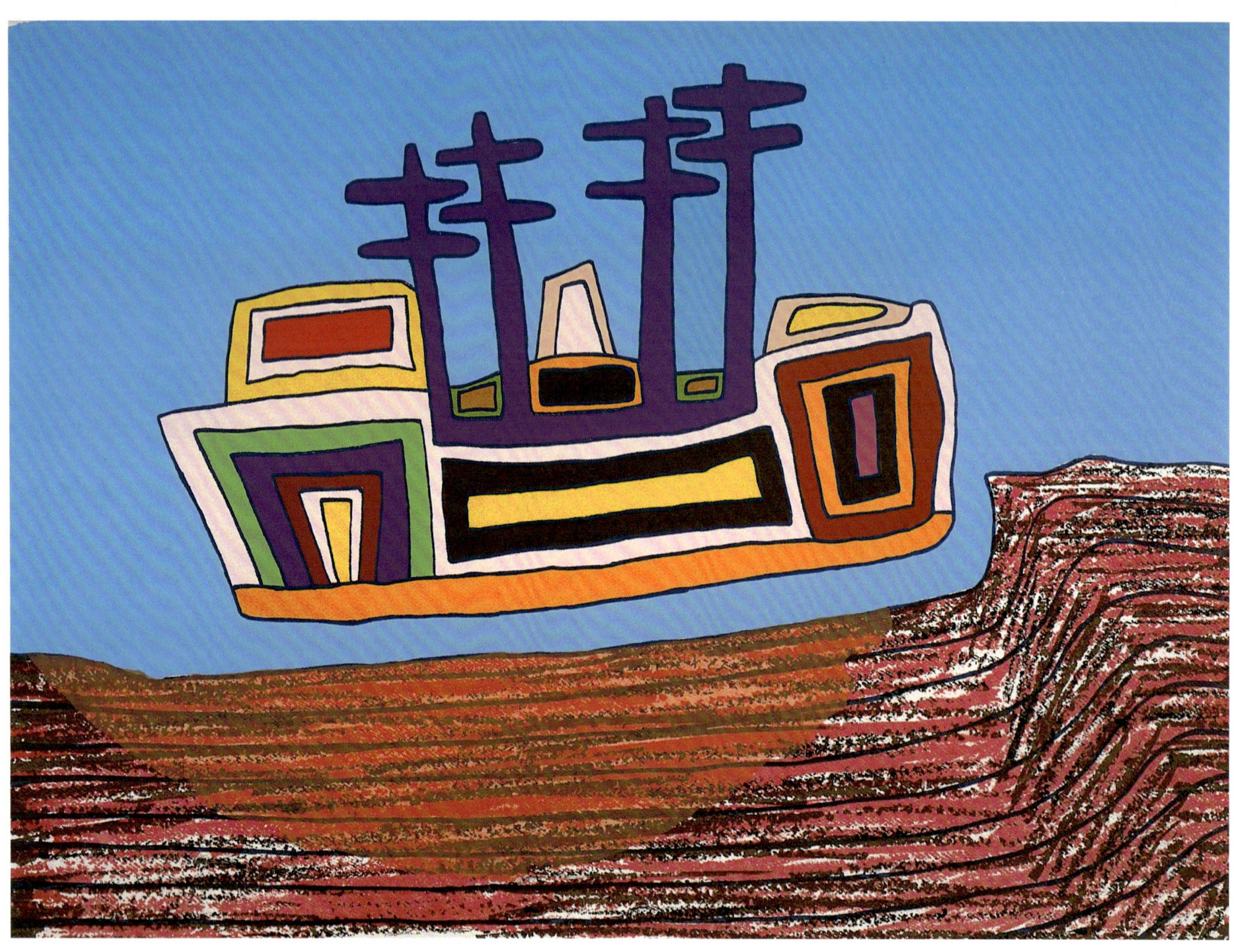

Kartiya Boat 1987
colour screen print
49.0 x 67.5 cm
Edition: 38/65

When the first *Kartiya* [Europeans] came to Australia with a
boat; when they first find Australia. That's a reef and land;
he's coming into that land.

Larripuka Main Country

1987
colour screen print
51.0 x 60.5 cm
Edition: 17/95

Because people been travel
through there Dreamtime,
big mob, right through to
Japingka they went past there.
That's the story of old people. Law country and
Dreamtime country. Oldtime,
people never been think
about anything. Everything
been change, like
Government come and talk
about what country people
want and people from bush,
they think back to go back to
country, like Dreamtime
country, grandfather country
and father country. Before,
people been live in the country and people been die in
the country, long time ago.
People move around, rainy
time, and when it come winter time, they move back
again.

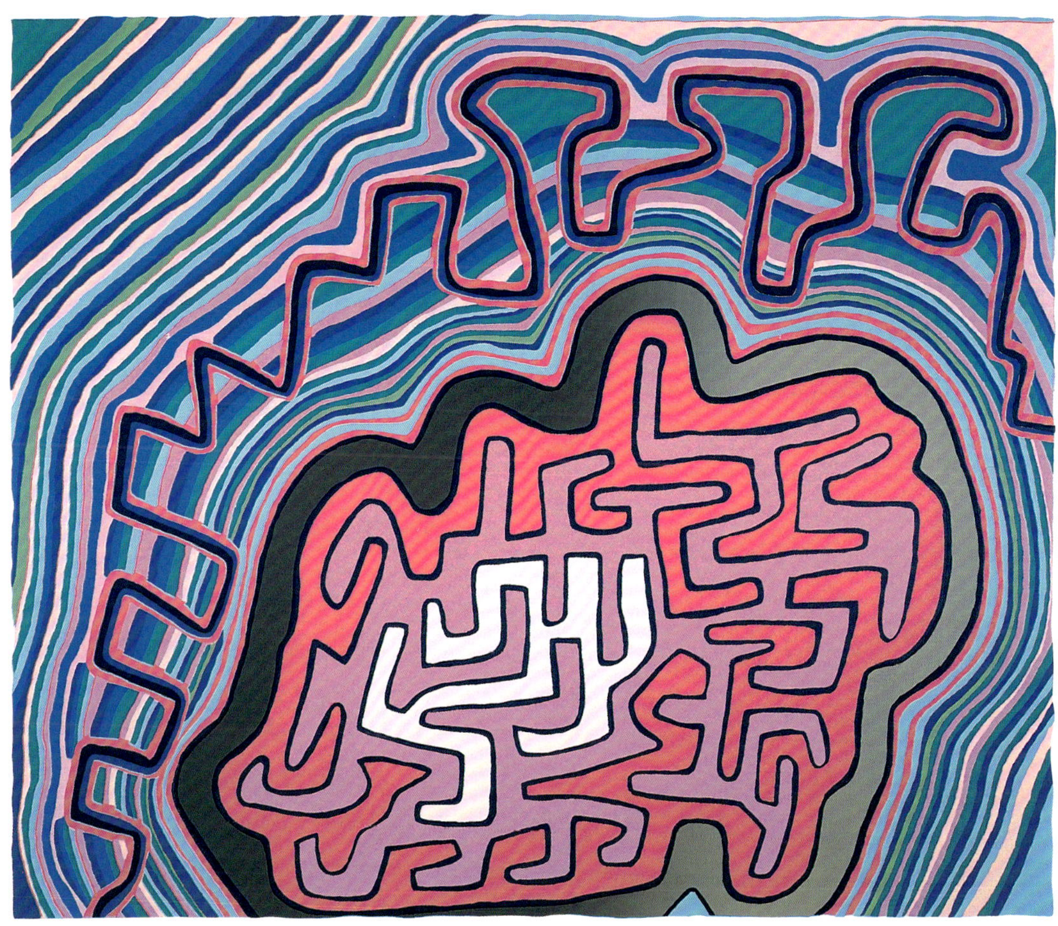

Kurntumaru and Parnaparnti I 1987

colour screen print
42.0 x 51.5 cm
Edition: 20/70

Kurntumaru and
Parnaparnti are two cousin
brothers. Dreamtime been
travelling west all round
the waterholes.

Yarlpurrulangu Karla Pirla
Yani Ngapawarla-
Ngapawarla

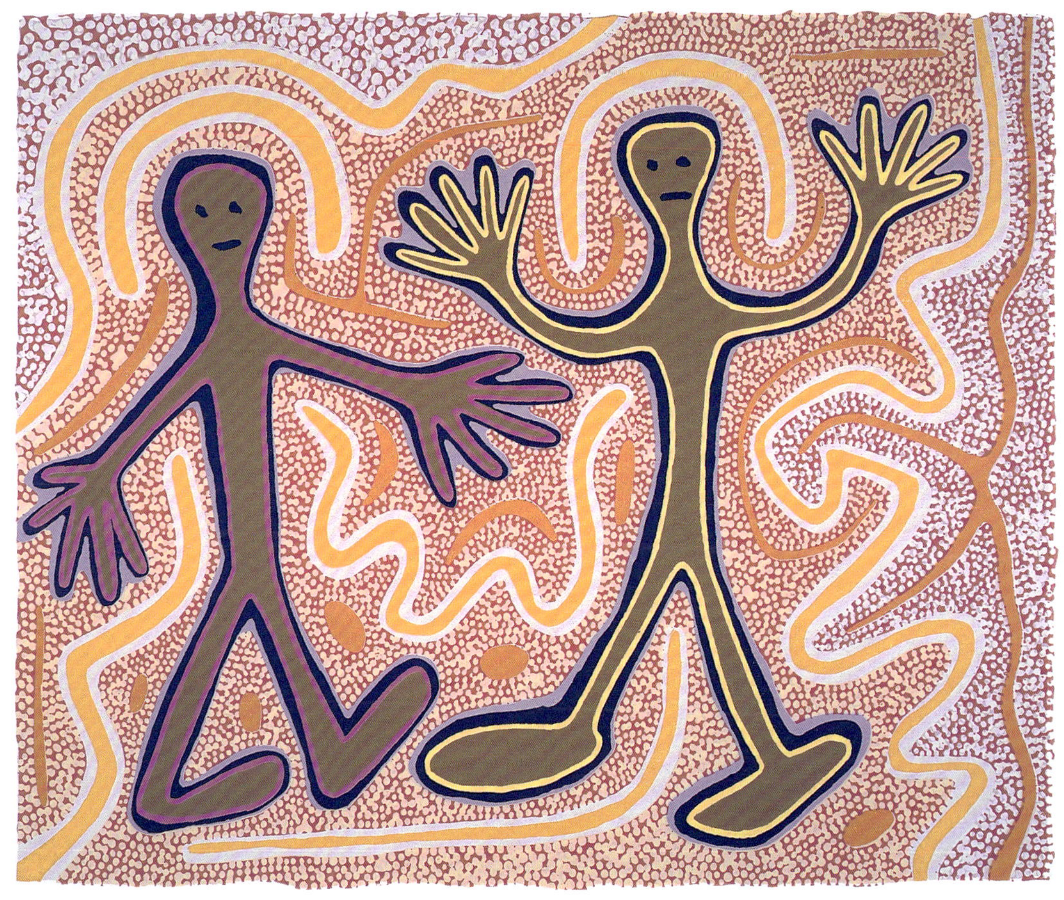

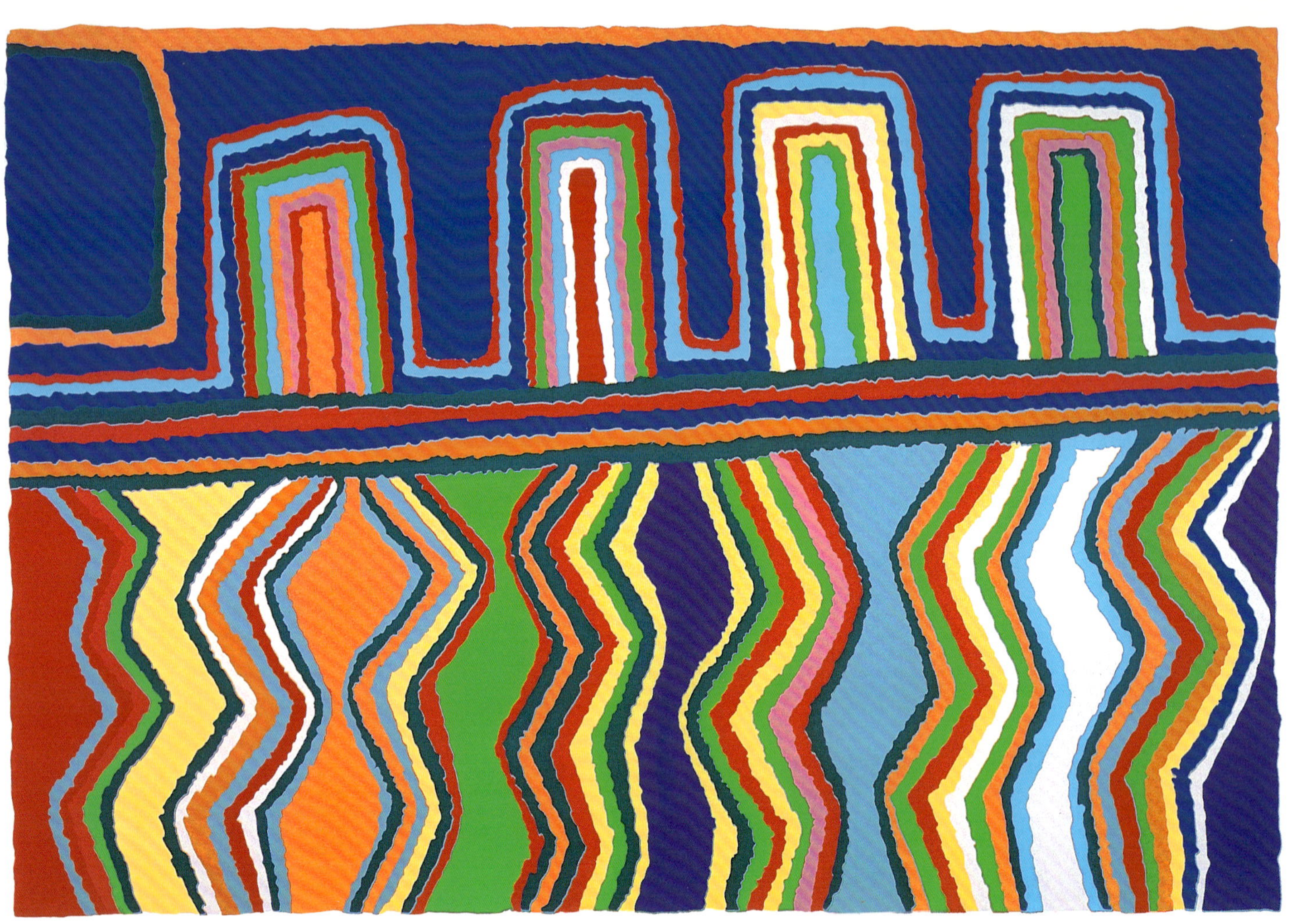

Thunderstorm   1987
colour screen print
50.5 x 76.5 cm
Edition: 19/85

Clouds and rain pouring.

Kurtukurtu, Ngangkaru, Waral

Pirnini Country III 1991
colour screen print
42.6 x 59.3 cm
Edition: 20/75

When the swans came up
to the billabong at *Pirnini*.
Sandhill country all around.

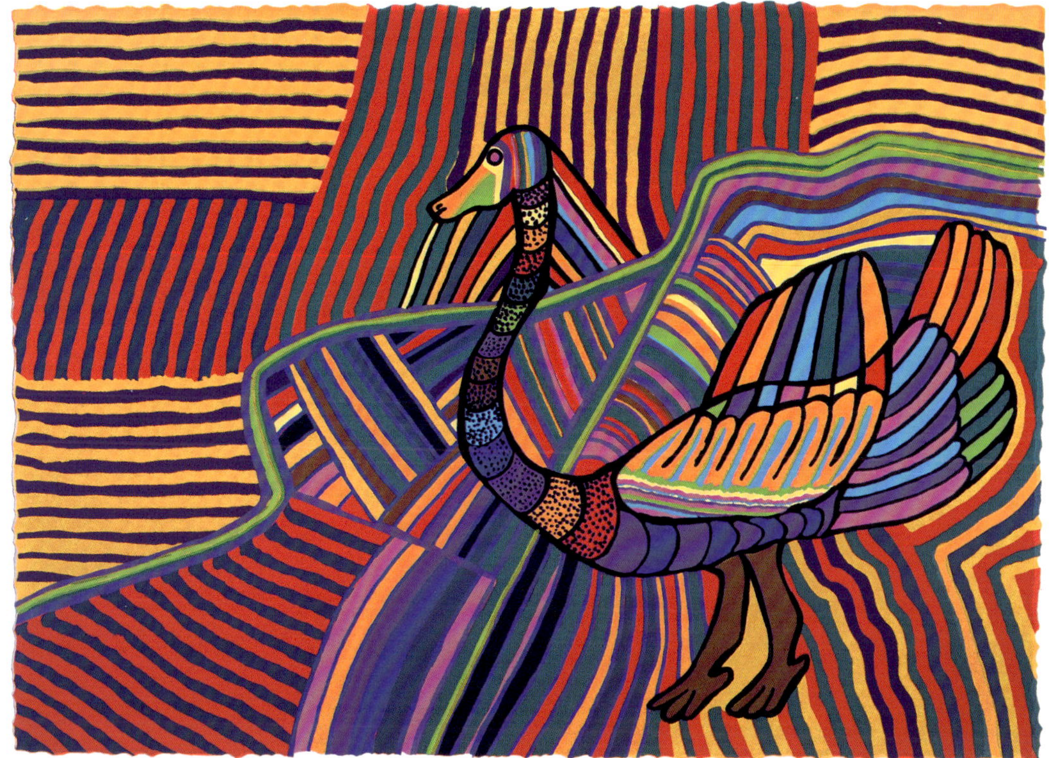

**Karnanganyja
and Likjartu** 1988
colour screen print
42.4 x 59.2 cm
Edition: 25/85

The story of the emu and
hawk. *Karnanganyja* [emu]
used to go hunting, kill all
the people for meat. Might
be big mob of kids. He used
to give cooked ones to his
cousins *Likjartu* [hawk] but
he never liked it. *Likjartu* eat
kangaroo and goanna, but he
feel sorry for these people.
Karnanganyja cooked some
people and went to sleep,
and *Likjartu* came and cut
off his arms while he was
asleep. That's why
Karnanganyja got tiny arms.
Karnanganyja dived into the
water and turned into a
snake. He put that lightning,
put on one side good one,
one side no good one. That's
law for rain. *Karnanganyja*
still make that noise like
water snake.

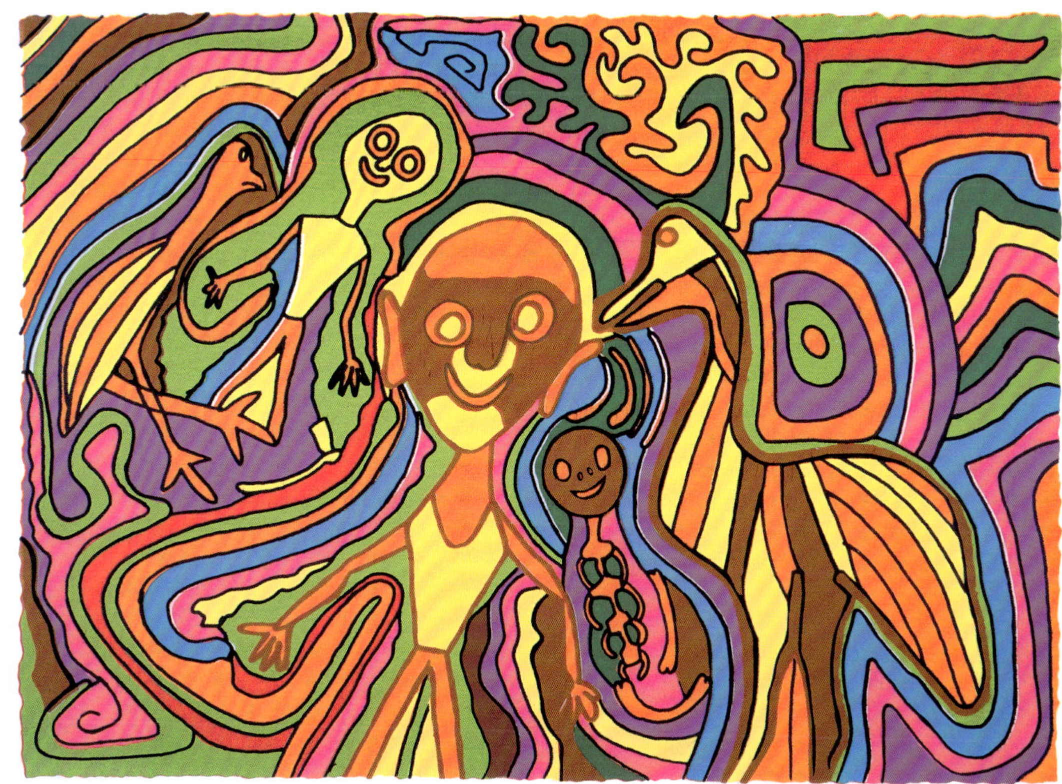

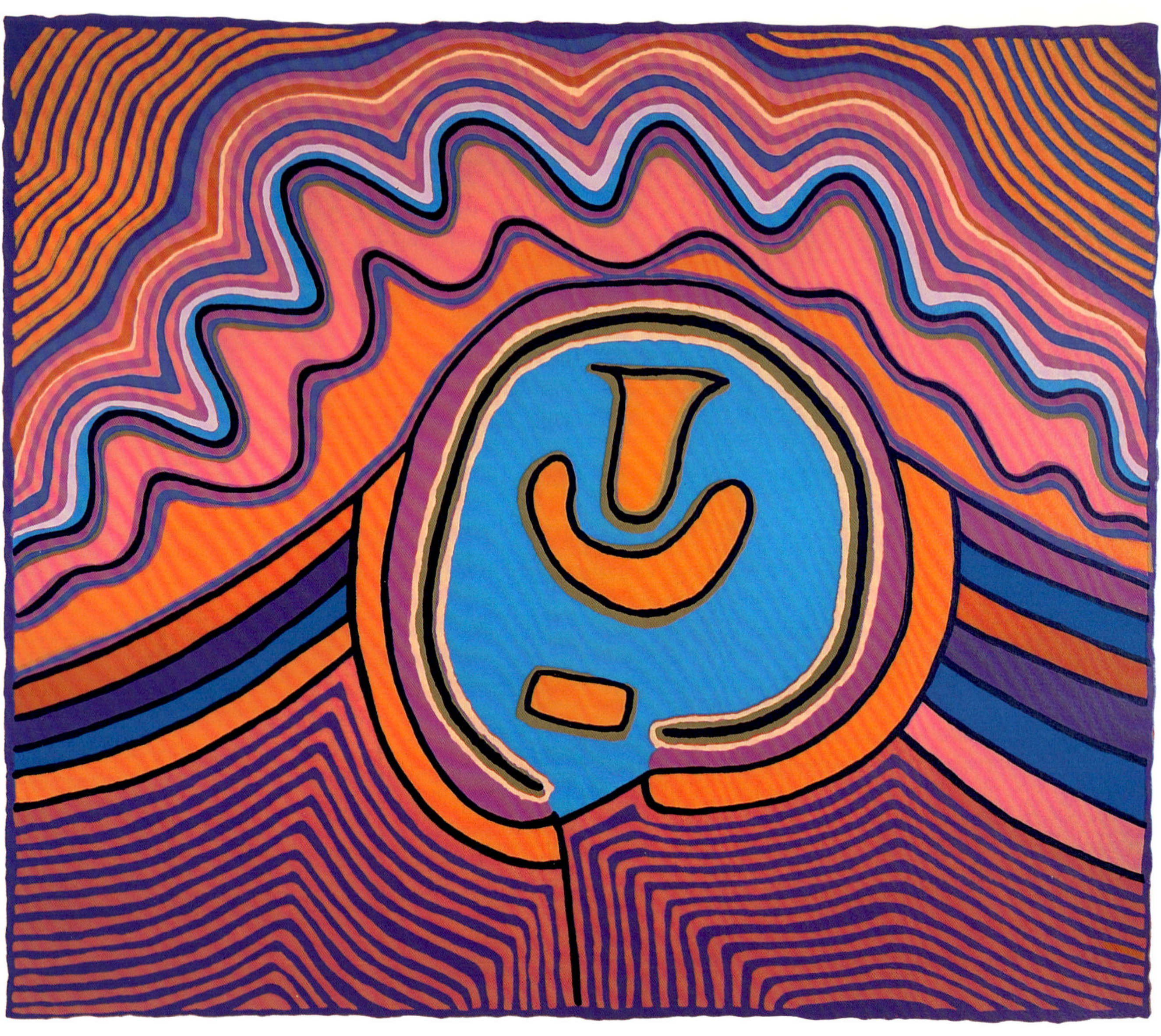

Grandfather and Grandson 1989
colour screen print
51.4 x 61.4 cm
Edition: 38/95

The grandfather starved the grandson for food. Every morning he went collecting yams and kept the good ones for himself and gave rubbish to his grandson. When the grandson went hunting he brought back goanna, bandicoot, snake and give them to his grandfather. One day the grandson went hunting and heard a *nyirin-nyirin* [beetle], he pulled up some grass and up shot water. He returned home and straight away big clouds came. The old man asked him what had he done. The grandson told him that he had been digging a waterhole so rain can come. They built a rock shelter but the old man told his grandson to lie outside and the big rain poured down all night. While the grandfather slept the young man grabbed the firestick and hid it in a rock hole in a cave.

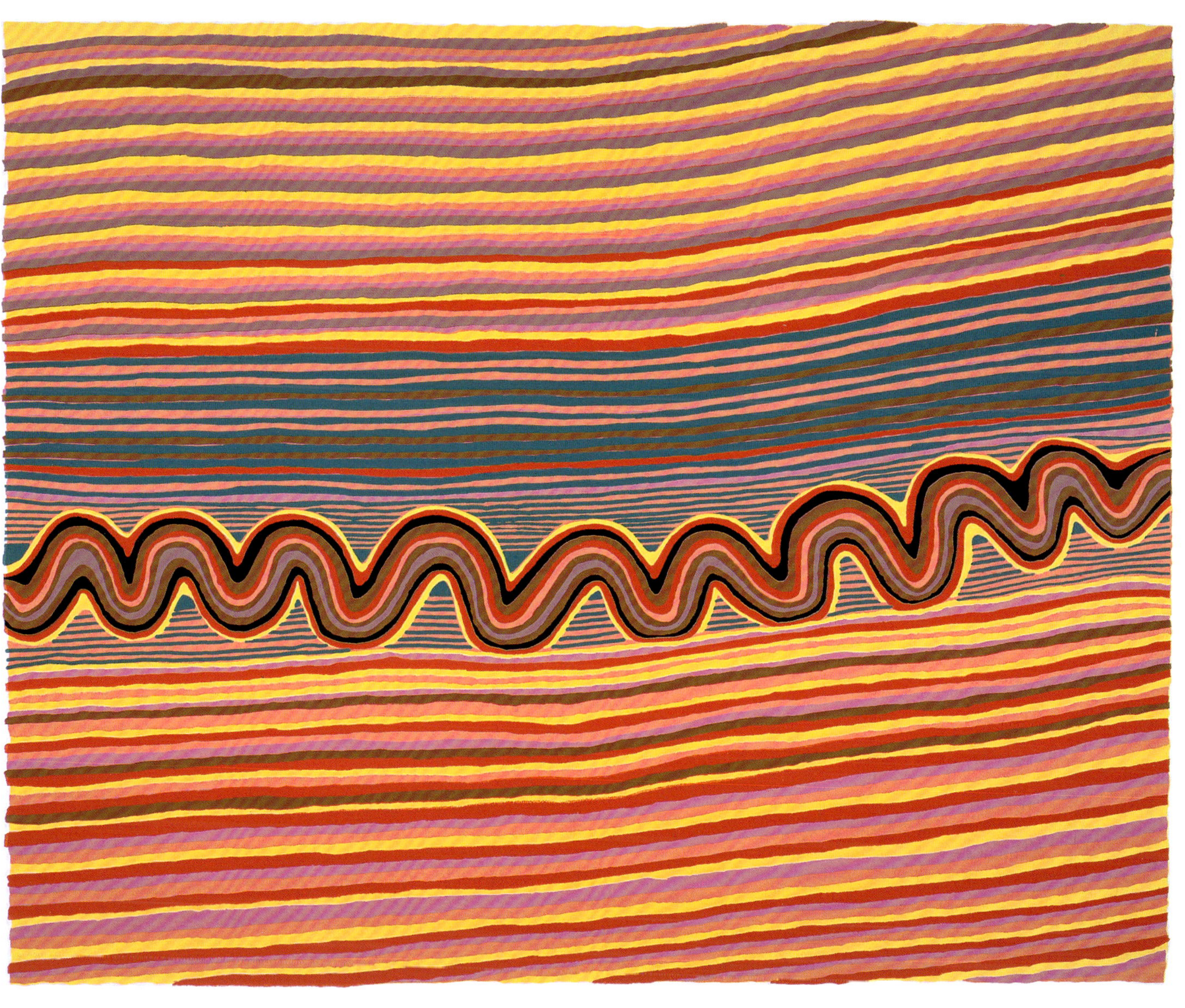

Yarntayi 1989
colour screen print
48.7 x 61.3 cm
Edition: 36/90

Two snakes been travelling Dreamtime through green
grass, sandhill on both sides. They make big track first,
then small track. They find big mob of people playing
corroboree, and the two fellas went round, one on each
side. They made the ground soft with their tails. The
people were in the middle like an island. The snakes made
the ground damp and sink down and drown all the people,
then they ate all the people. Then they keep going. They
make a camp and sink down in the water on two sides,
one good one, one salty one. When they been go they been
make a camp right there. That's country for *Looma* people.

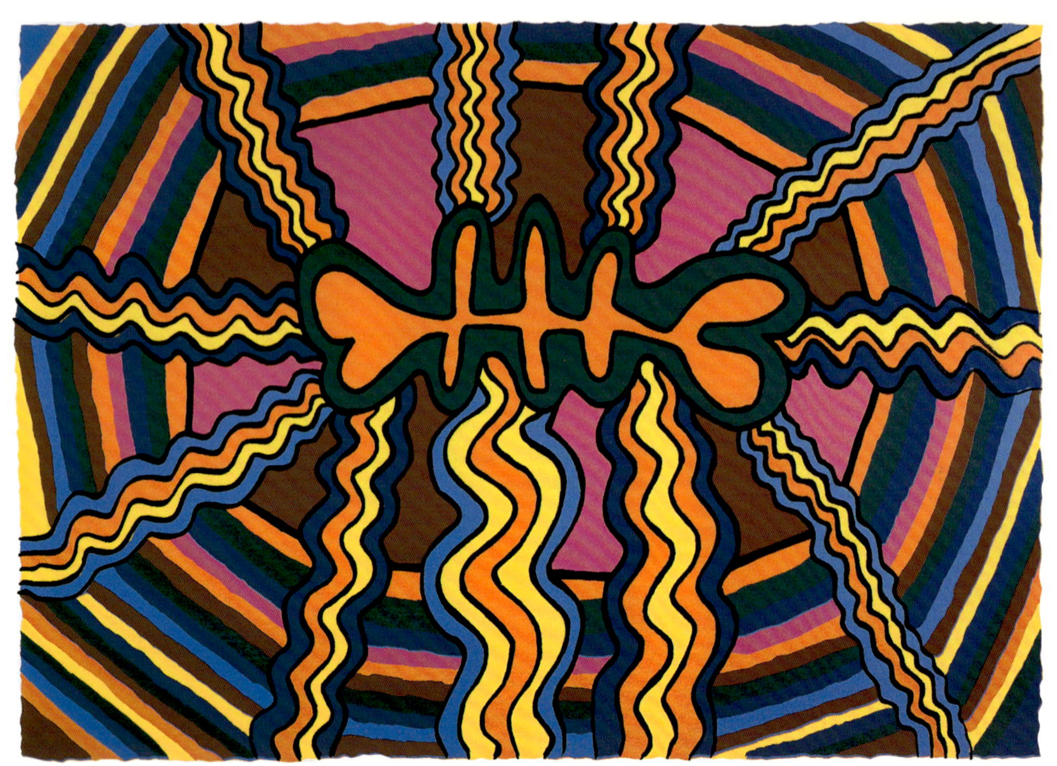

Japingka Country
1989
colour screen print
45.6 x 65.0 cm
Edition: 22/80

Waterhole and *jilji* country.
Before, the *Kurtukurtu*
came over here. That's
rainclouds. Then the
Kurtukurtu turned into
all the *jilji* – turned into
sandhills all round here.

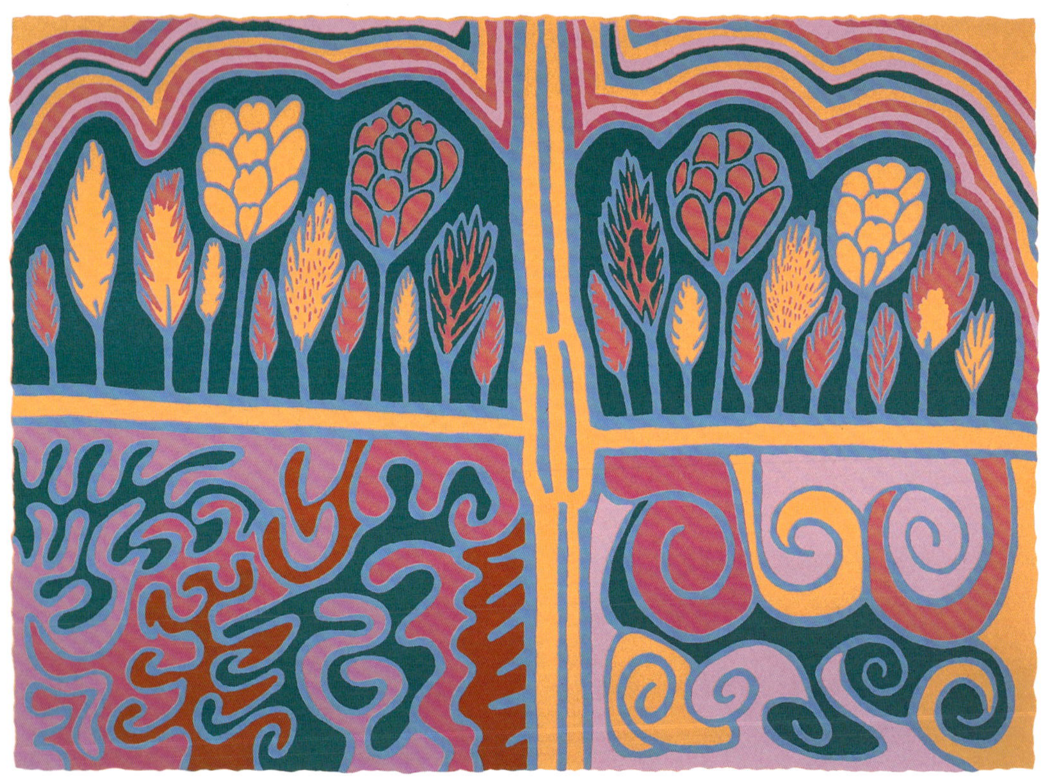

Country 1989
colour screen print
42.4 x 59.8 cm
Edition: 26/95

Desert flowers after rain.
Flowers growing in the
desert, in the dry weather.
Wattles grow in June and
July. Some grow after rain.

Jila Japingka 1991
colour screen print
42.0 x 59.4 cm
Edition: 35/95

There is a snake right there
at *Japingka* waterhole.
Sometime when he get
there, he's laying in a tree.
Kalpurtu is the more powerful one. He's got a strong
wind, hail and dust storm.
Jutul is a dust storm, a
strong one. *Karliwiji* is a big
wind, more strong, can
blow down big trees and
all like a cyclone.
Ngartiwara is smoke coming up from the ground, a
white one, comes up before
rain. *Pulijita* is a hail storm,
it can pull out the grass,
make the tree with no leaf
or bark. It can kill animals.
The people can go under-
ground, like in a cave.
There it can't touch them.

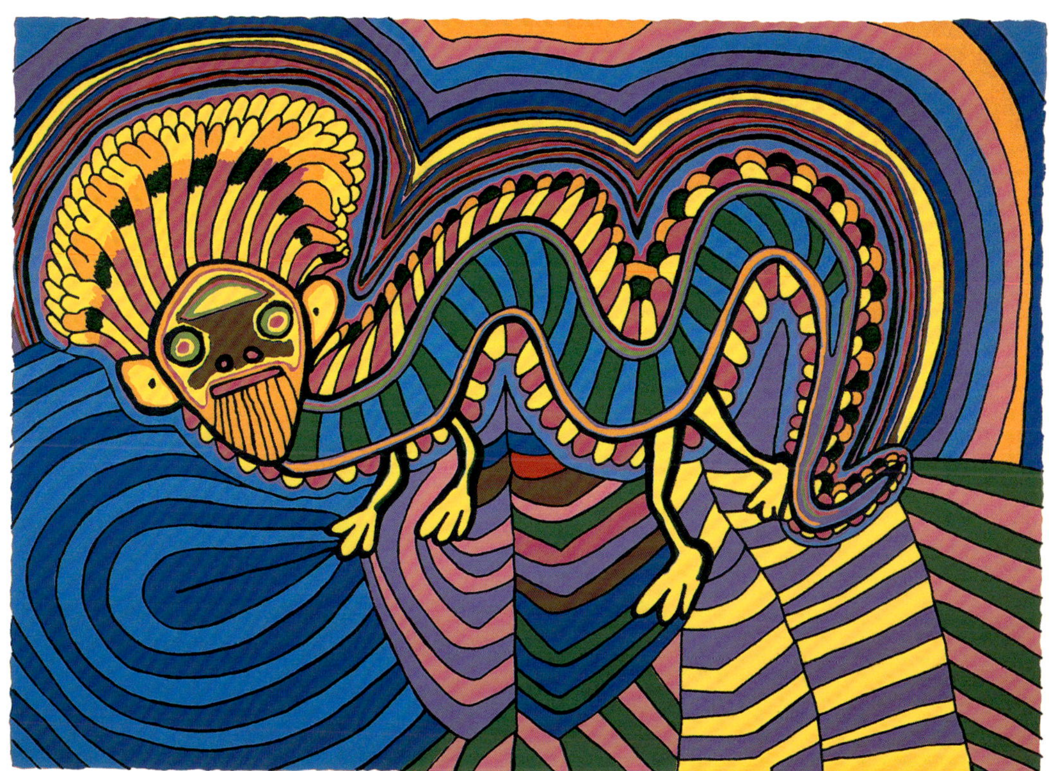

Jurtirangu – Rainbow
1989
colour screen print
51.7 x 61.1 cm
Edition: 19/95

This is the rainbow
coloured watersnake,
travelling in a thunder-
storm. He's travelling near
Japingka waterhole, and
he's got *Kurtukurtu* all
round. *Kurtukurtu*, that's
rain clouds. They call that
watersnake *Kalpurtu*.

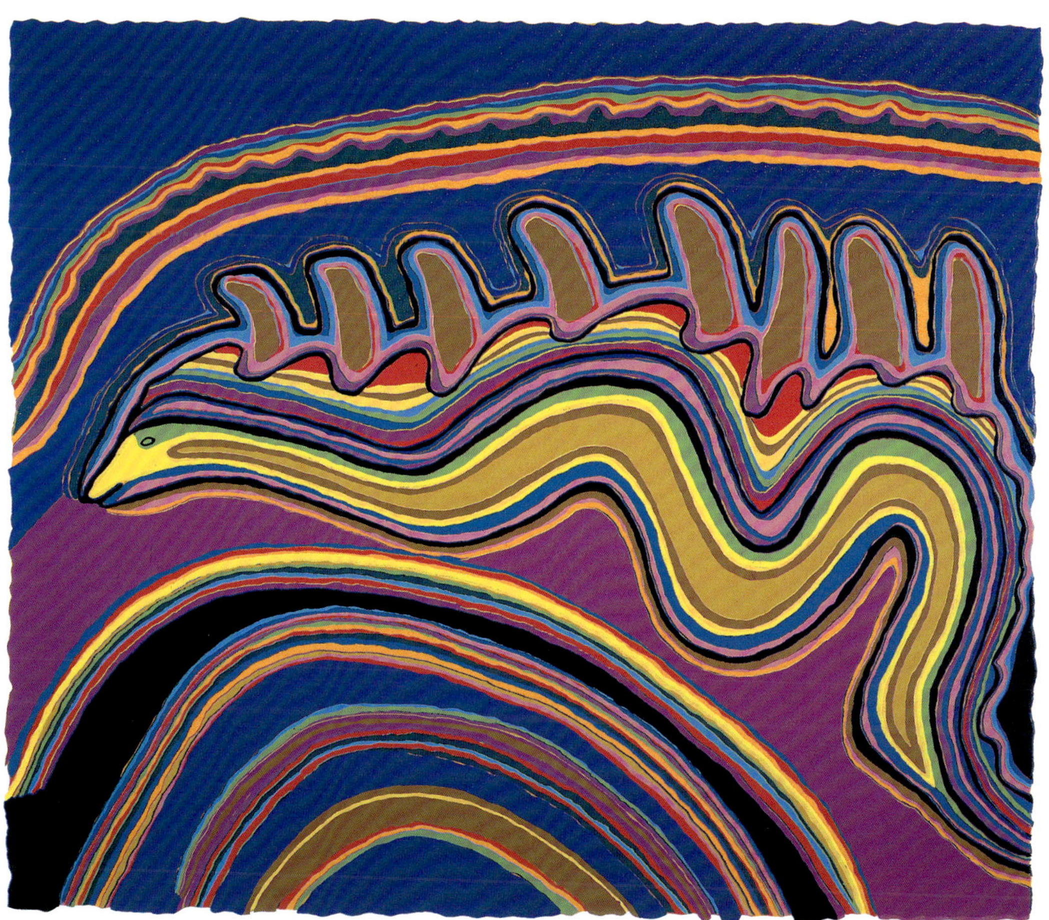

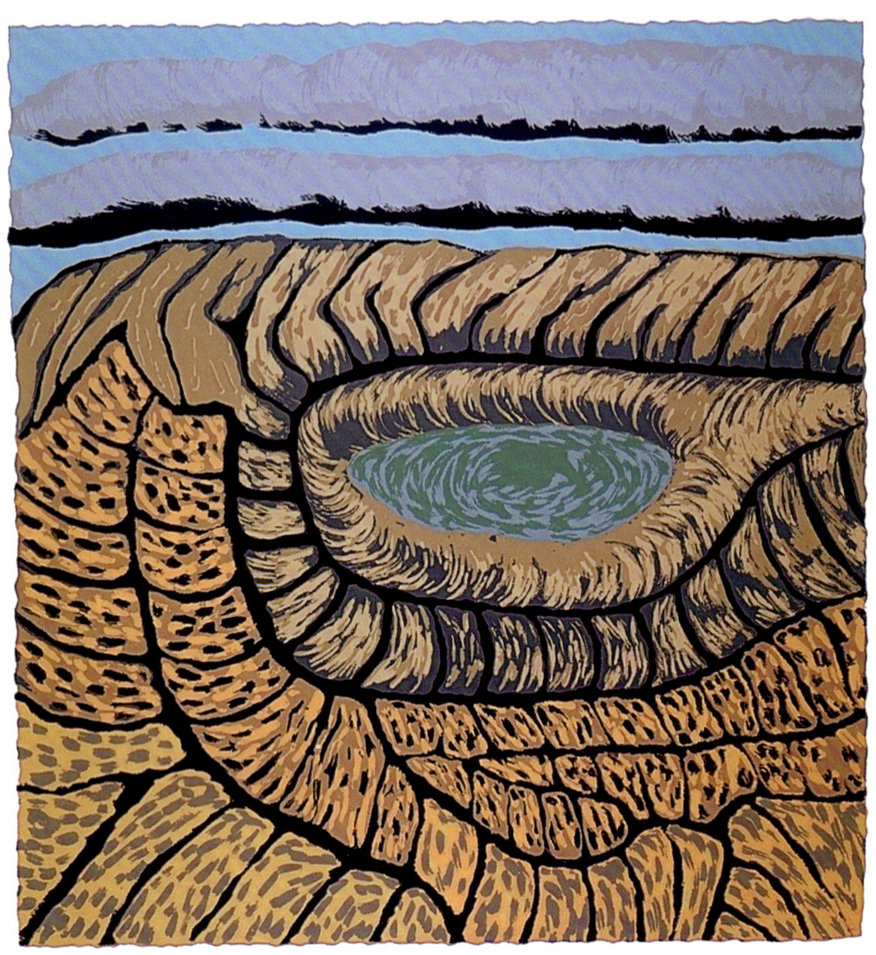

Jarrngajartu Rockhole
1991
colour screen print
52.7 x 50.3 cm
Edition: 68/95

People used to go to that rockhole before. All the desert people used to go there, from *Rinjarr*. It's not far from where we live now.

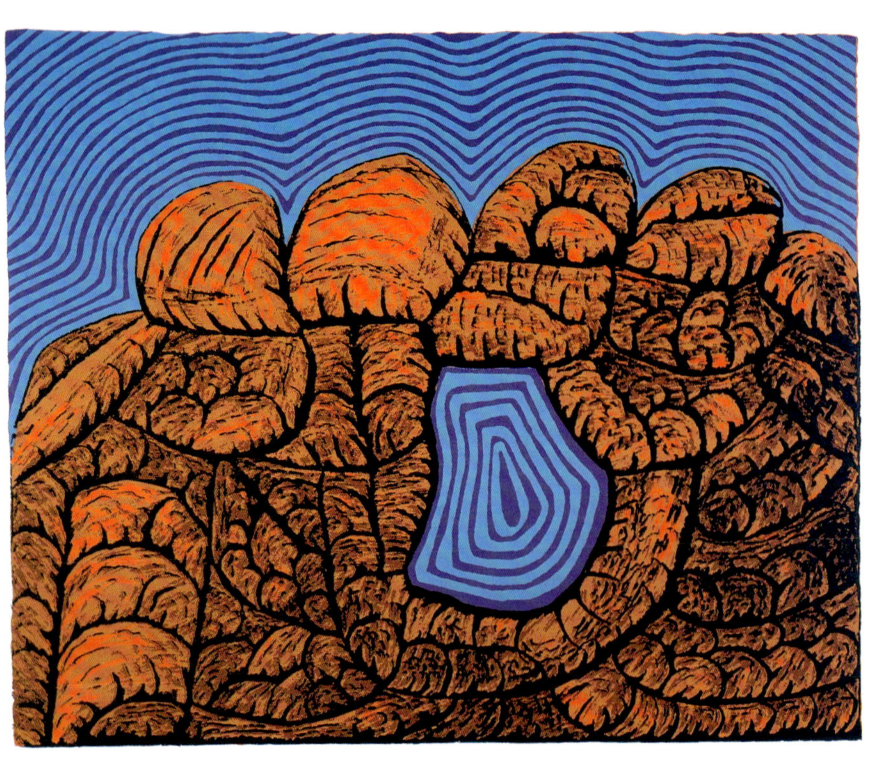

Father's Country – Selling Stock 1991
colour screen print
40.7 x 50.9 cm
Edition: 50/95

When the two cousin brothers, *Kurntumaru* and *Parnaparnti*, travelled through there, they been looking back. They find hole right through, like a cave. They seen right through the rock.
The country goes higher. That's my father's country.

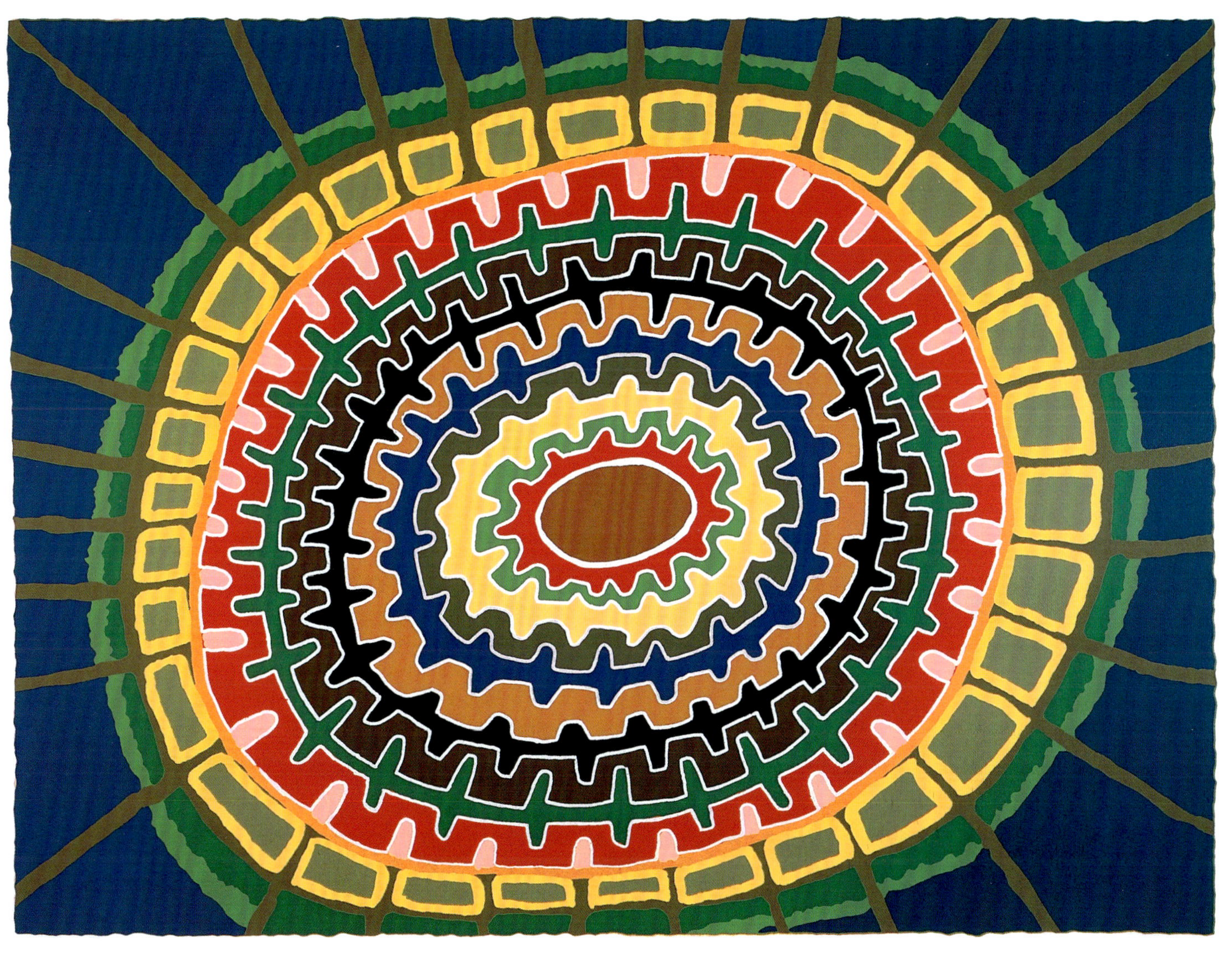

Japingka Jila 1989
colour screen print
56.3 x 76.2 cm
Edition: 19/95

Japingka is a big waterhole. The people tell the Spirit Snake
to look after this place and bring rain. People all stand up
all round, that's a big law. After that, the *Linjirr* comes up.
That's small clouds, in a long line. When you see that long
line of clouds, that means rain is coming up.

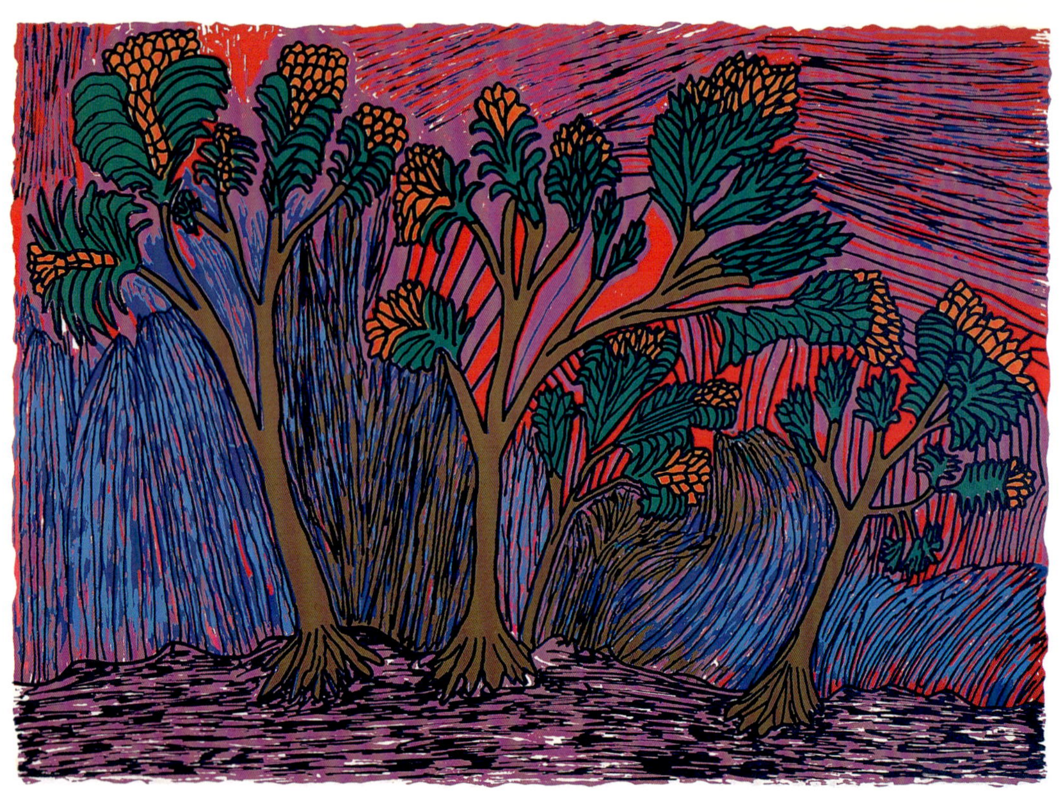

Afternoon Light 1989
colour screen print
42.0 x 59.5 cm
Edition: 25/95

Afternoon time, the sun going down, with light shining through bush peanut trees, on rocks and long grass after rain. This is *warla*, lake, *jiwarri*, billabong and *wirrkuja*, little rockhole, country.

Karawarra Lurra Karla Tartayan Jangkala

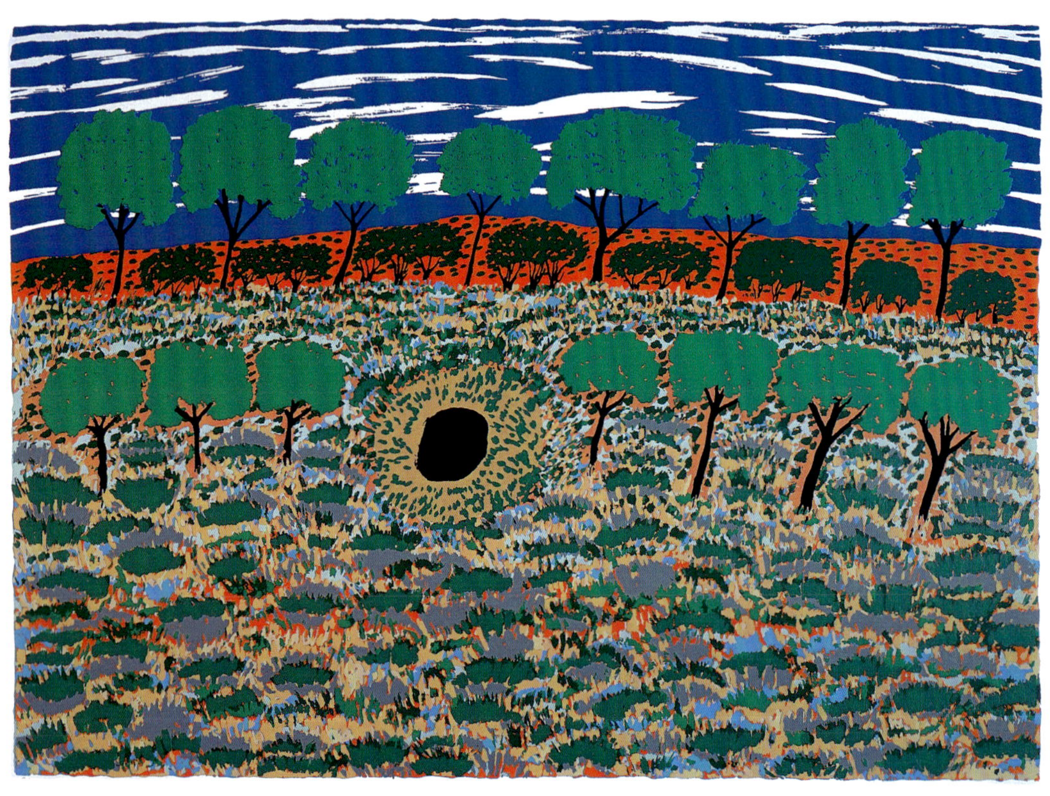

Jumu Yirrjirn 1991
colour screen print
42.2 x 59.5 cm
Edition: 21/95

Jumu is like a seasonal waterhole. This *jumu* is in the *Japingka* area. The big dark trees all around are bush peanut trees. In my country there we eat the peanuts, cook them in the fire and open them up.

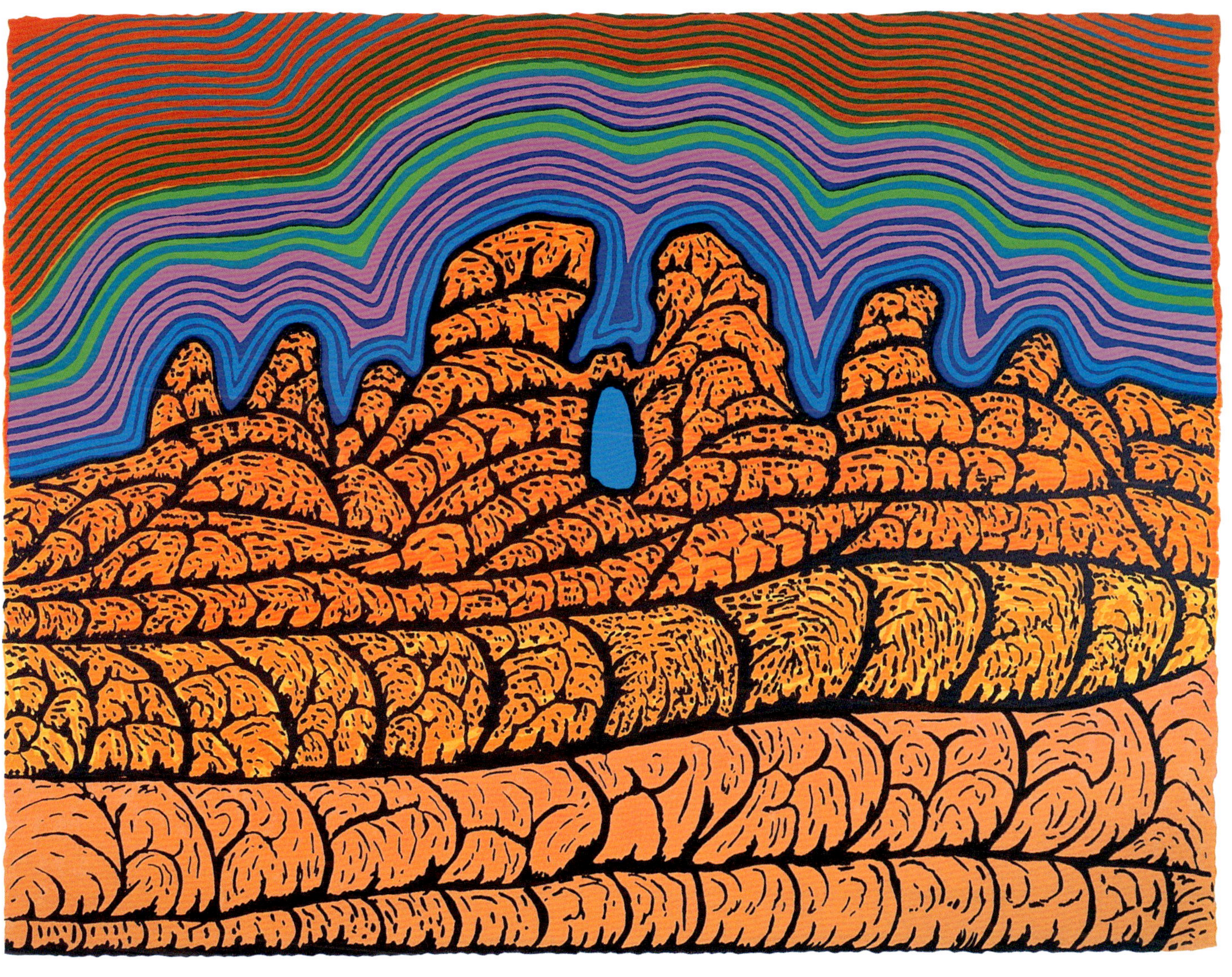

Kurriny Piyirnkujarra 1991
colour screen print
48.2 x 64.8 cm
Edition: 42/95

Story of the two men they been see right through that hill.
That's other side *Japingka* waterhole, not far from *Nurtu*.

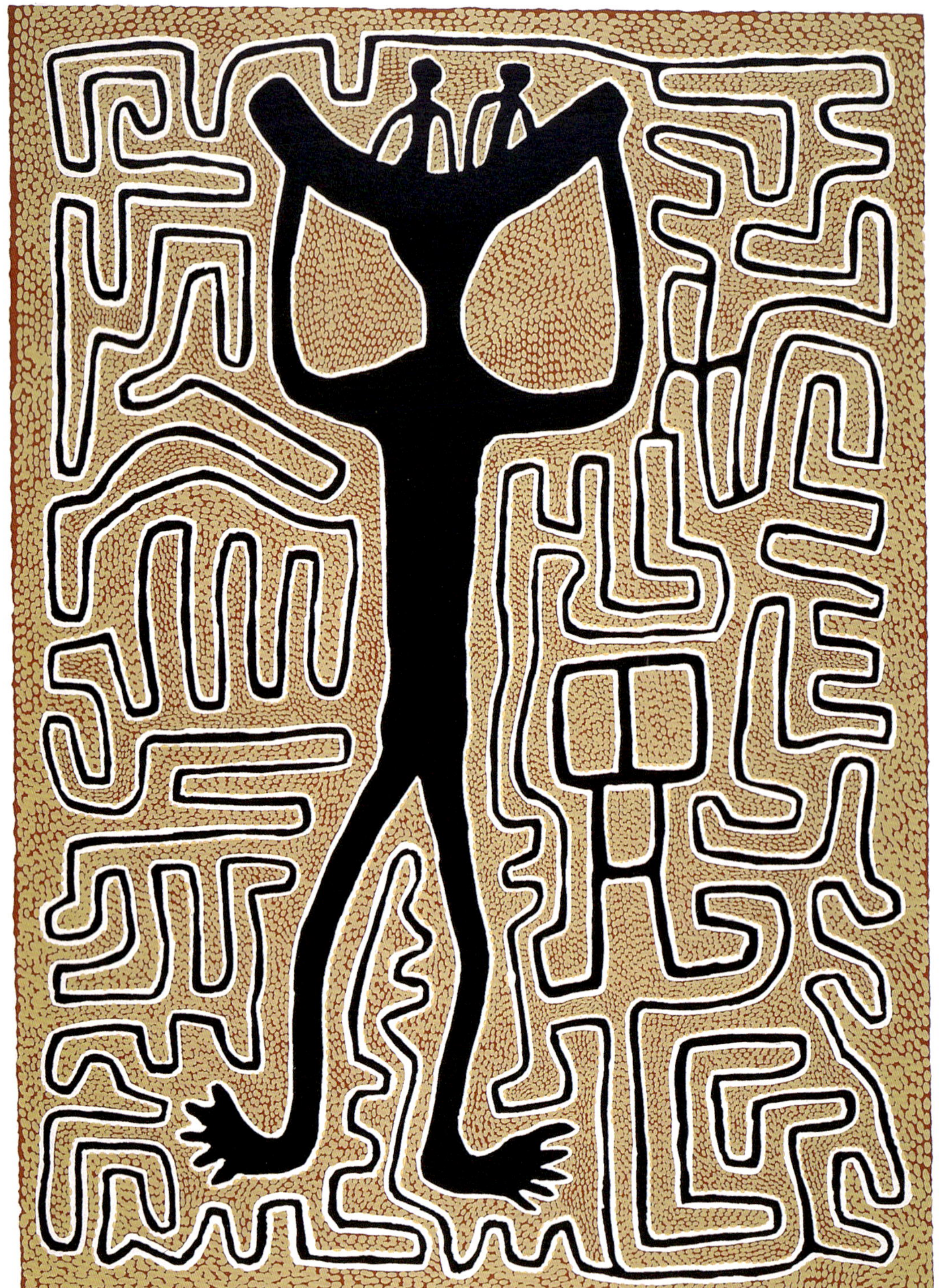

Woman Carrying Her Two Boys 1991
colour screen print
76.0 x 55.7 cm
Edition: 63/95

A woman was bringing her two sons from the south. One day she left them at a waterhole. She went hunting. A big mob of women were chasing the two men, and made them very sick. The mother of the two men came back and found them lying there worn out. She picked them up and carried them in a coolamon, carried them all the way to *Junjuwarnti*, on top of her head. She was watching her two sons. All the women came and asked for the two men. At that waterhole *Junjuwarnti* you can see all the trees where all the women came out of the scrub. The mother told them to go back, and took off with her two sons. There are double waterholes all along that way. The two boys died later, at *Pukapuka* and *Kujinuru*, two waterholes close together. That's in my country.

Parnanytu Pinya Kangani Walakujarra

Kalpurtu II 1991
colour screen print
76.2 x 55.5 cm
Edition: 43/95

That's *Japingka* waterhole.
Two *Kalpurtu* are standing
up; they got up from the
waterhole. *Kalpurtu* are
magic snakes. When they
smell people, they get up
from the waterhole.

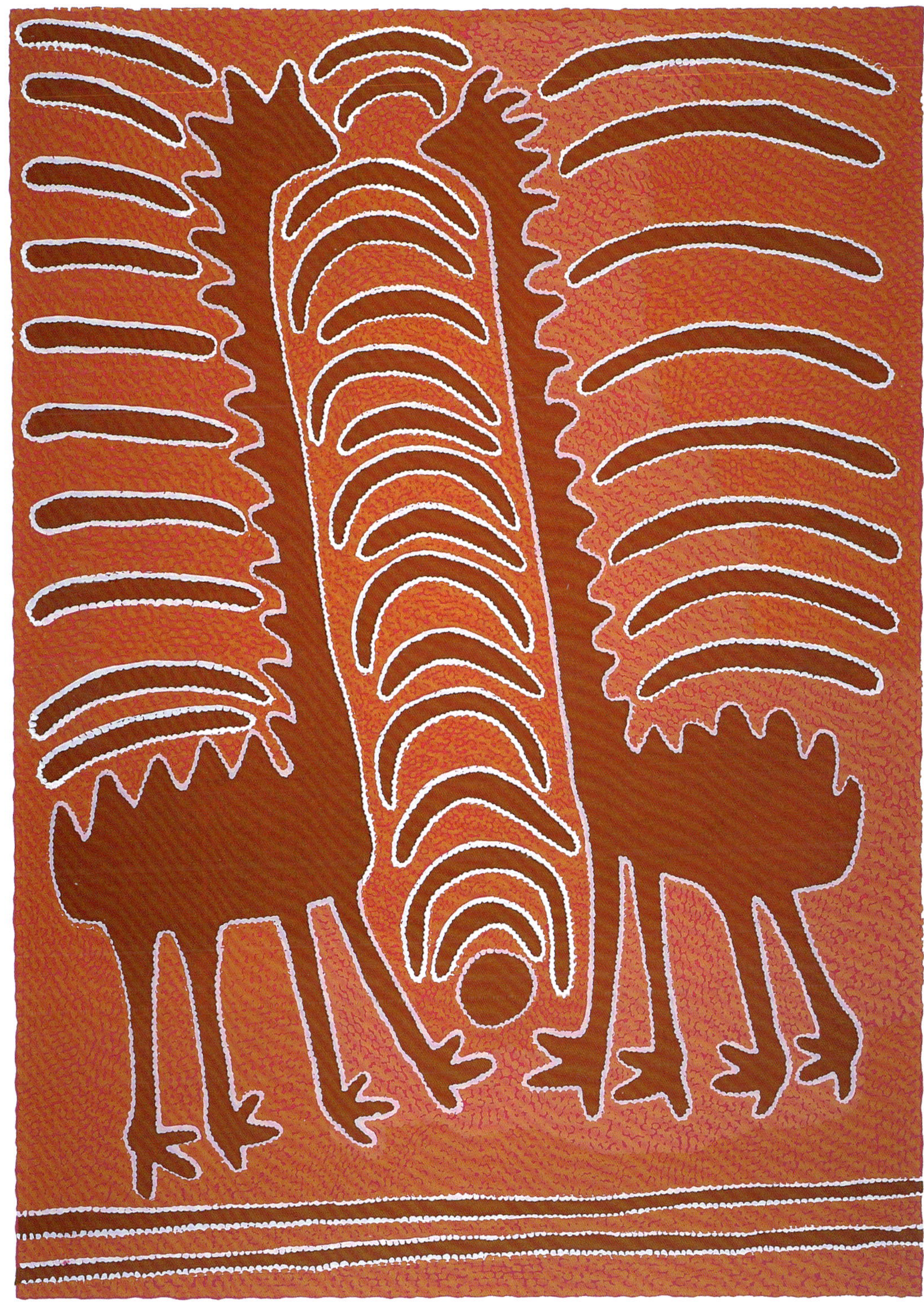

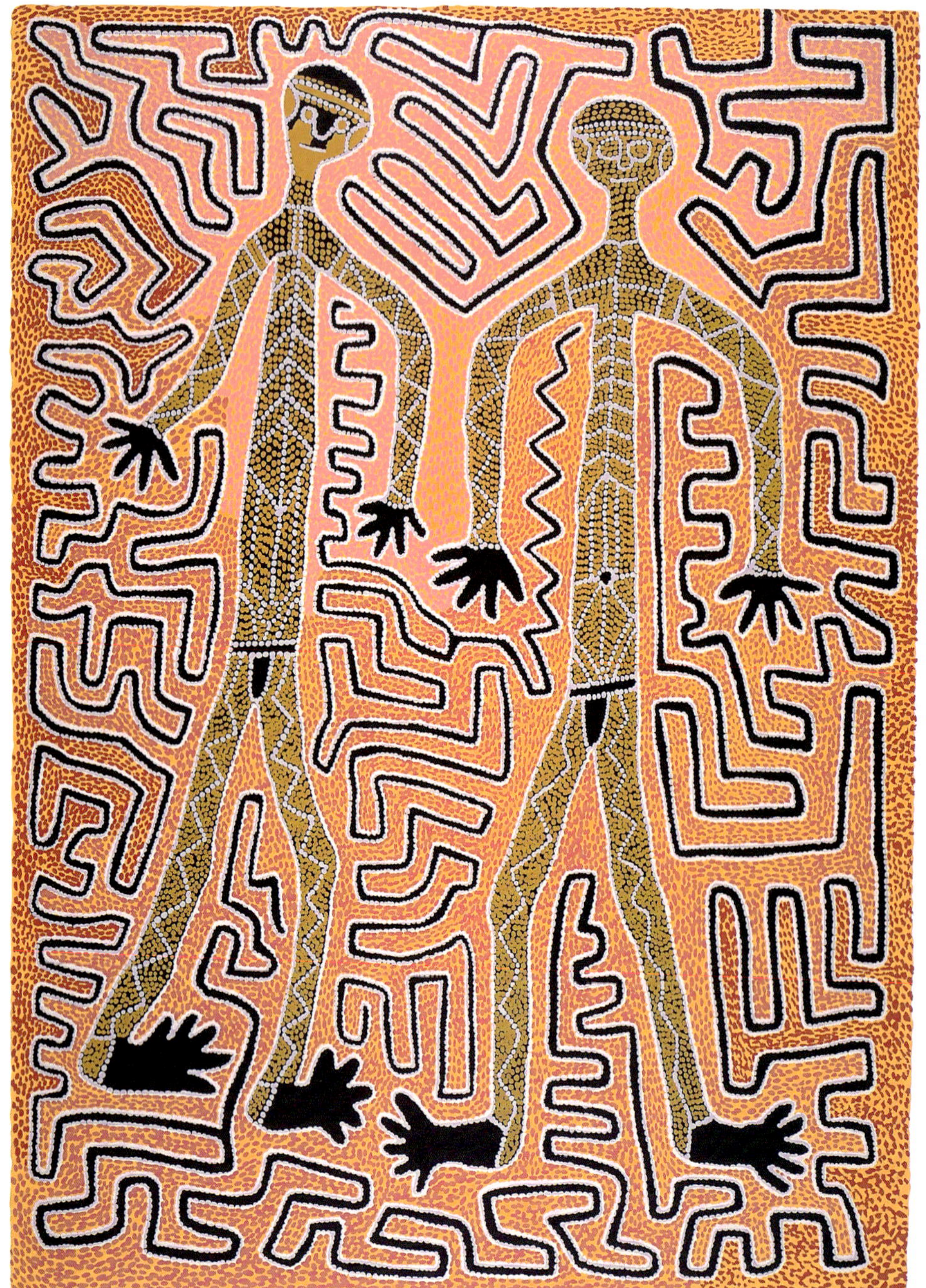

**Kurntumaru and
Parnaparnti III** 1991
colour screen print
75.3 x 55.0 cm
Edition: 57/95

Parnaparnti is the yellow
sand goanna and
Kurntumaru is the black
goanna that hides in the
trees. In the Dreamtime,
these two were cousin-
brothers. They were walk-
ing round like men, big
men and strong, not like
people today. They started
off a long way east, and
they travelled west. But
they didn't travel in a
straight line. They went up
and down, north and
south, back again on the
way. They went straight
through the desert and
they came out at the salt
water, in Broome country.
That's an important story
for the old people from all
over. As they travelled, the
two men saw different
places and they gave them
names. They met people
and snakes and they saw
birds and animals, and
they gave them all names.
These were the first people
and animals. They were
big. Ordinary people came
after.

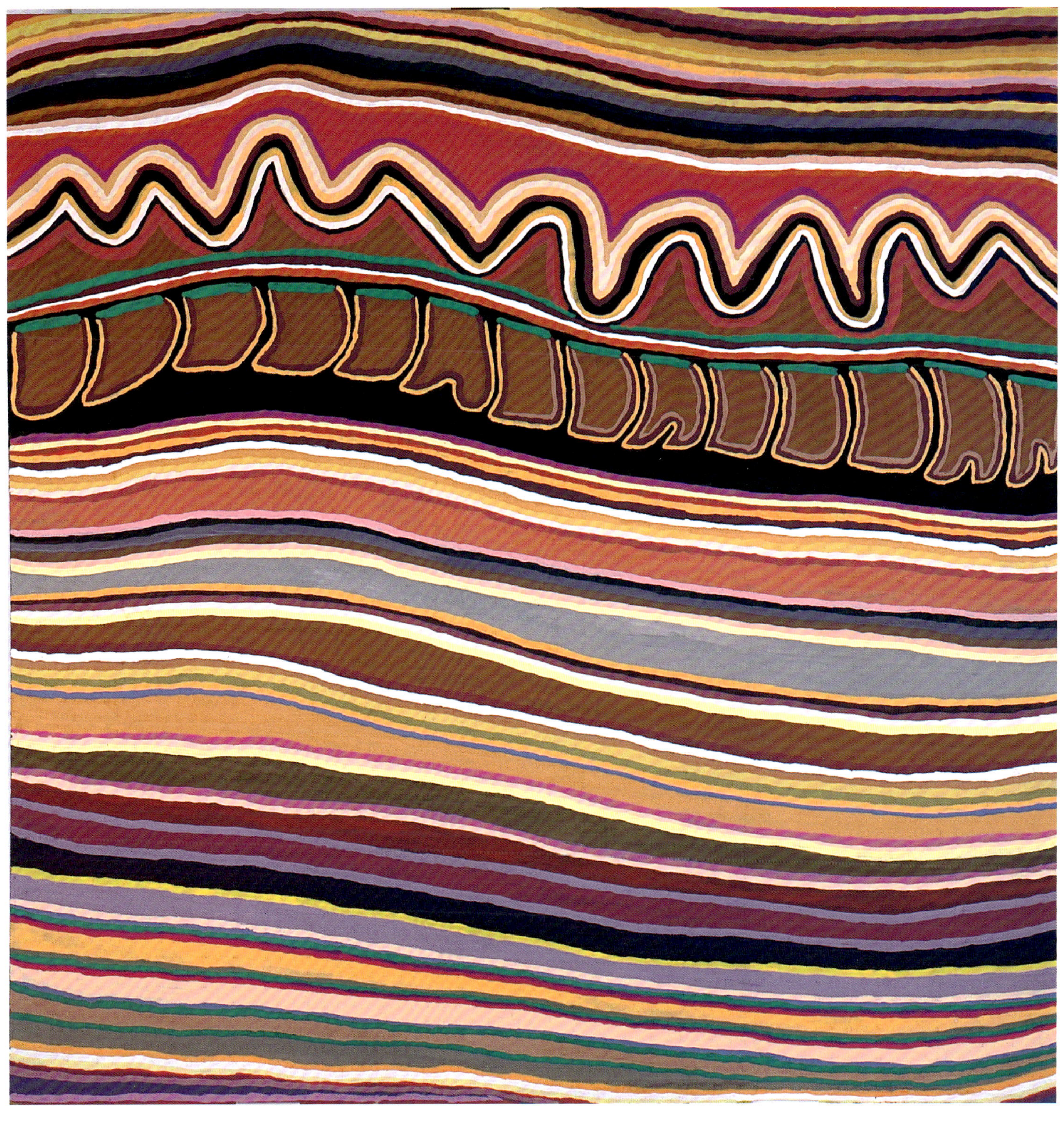

Sandhills in the Simpson Desert 1984
gouache on Masonite
122.0 x 122.5 cm

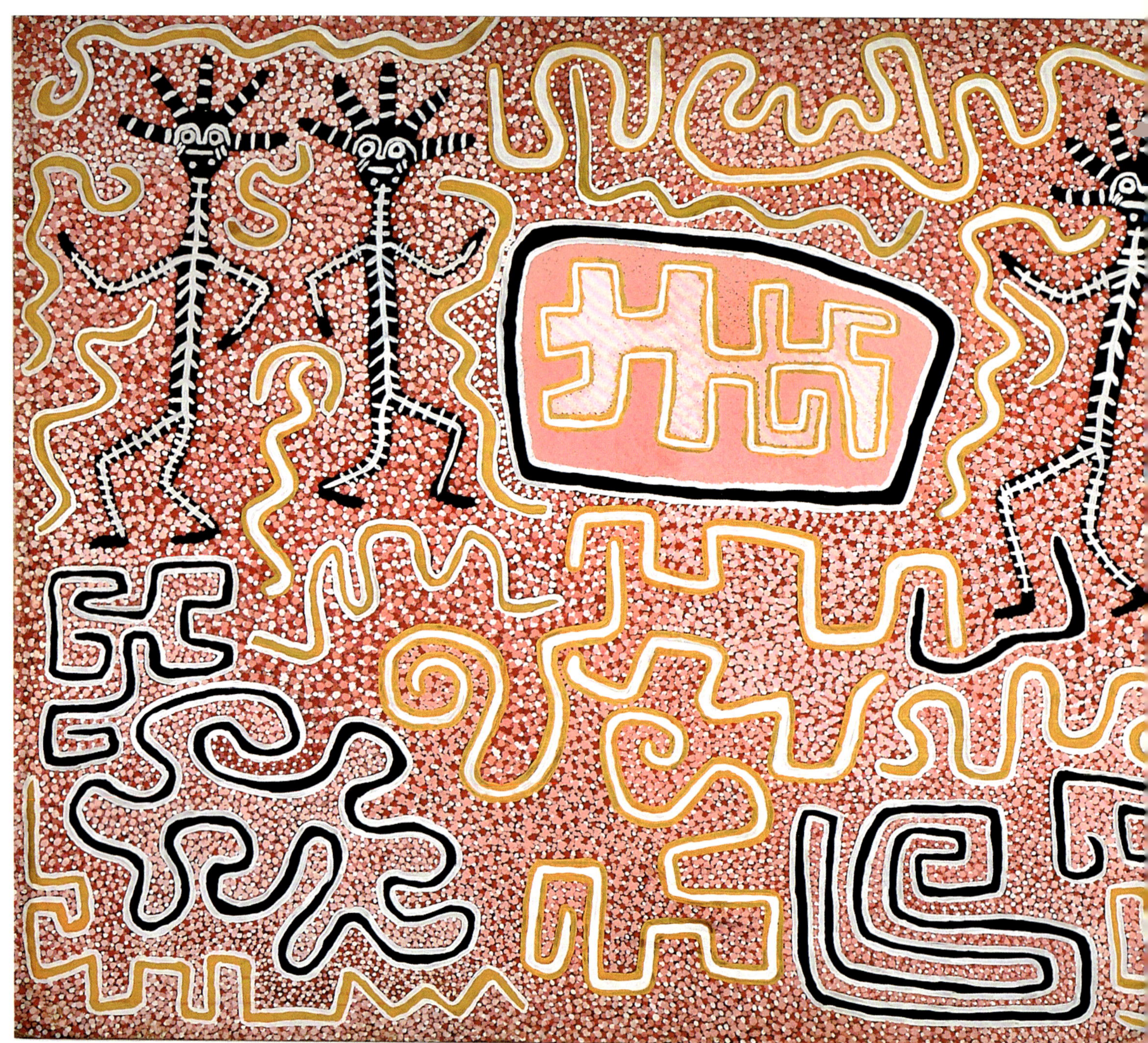

Untitled c.1980
acrylic on Masonite
90.0 x 180.0 cm

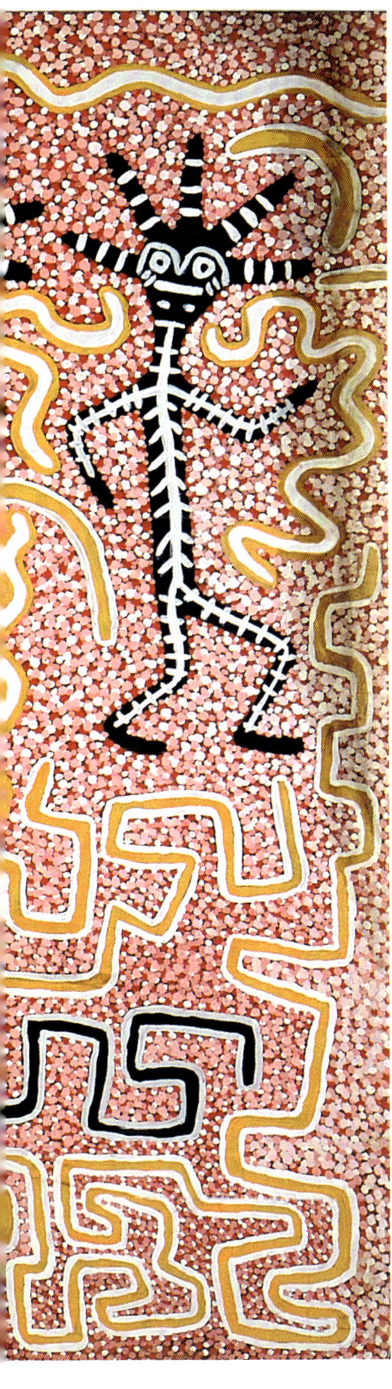

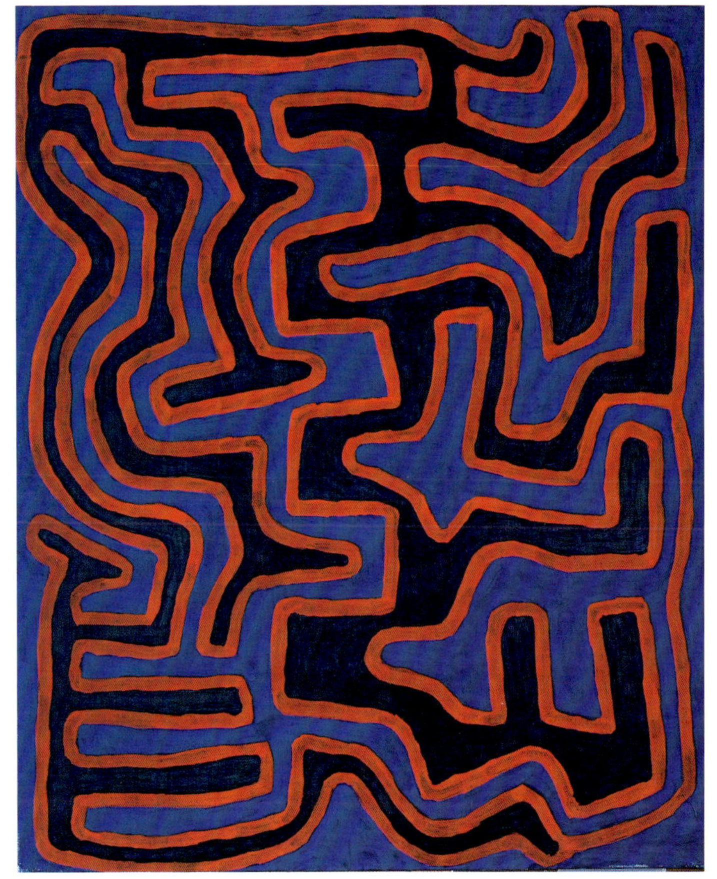

Jilji Country 1987
acrylic on canvas
60.8 x 50.7 cm

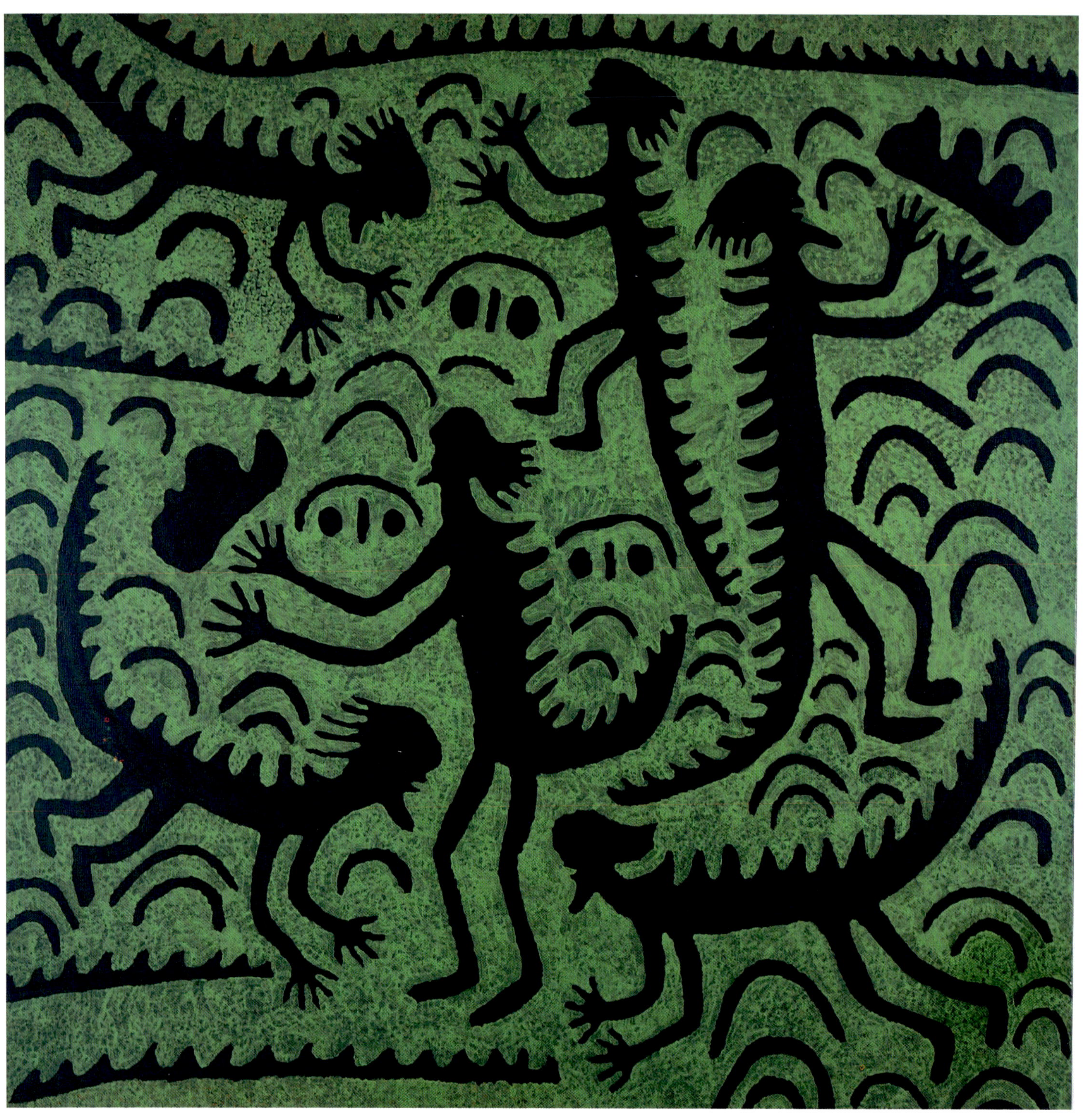

Japingka waterhole 1987
acrylic on canvas
123.5 x 123.0 cm

**Kurntumaru and
Parnaparnti** 1991
acrylic on canvas
164.0 x 117.5 cm

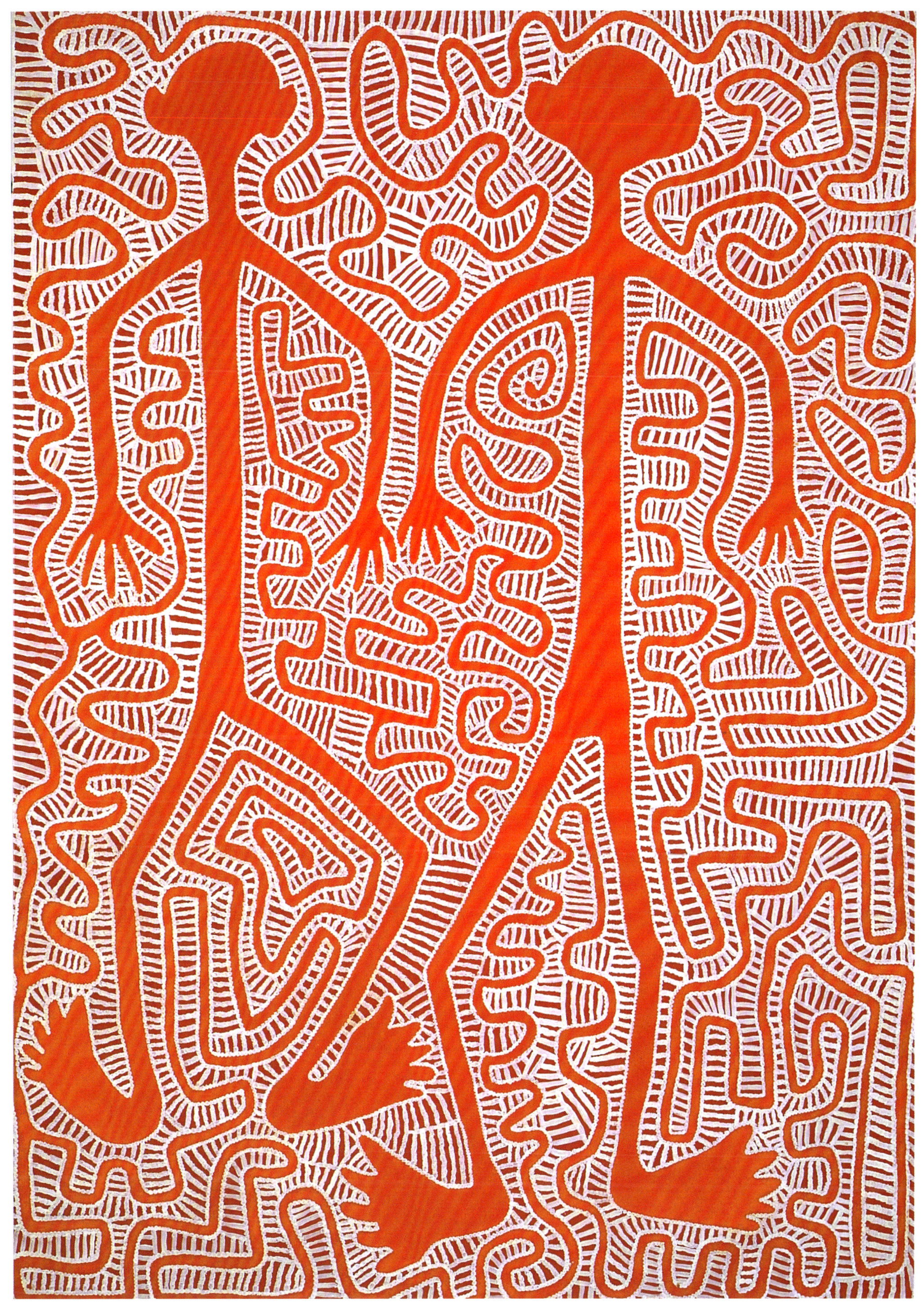

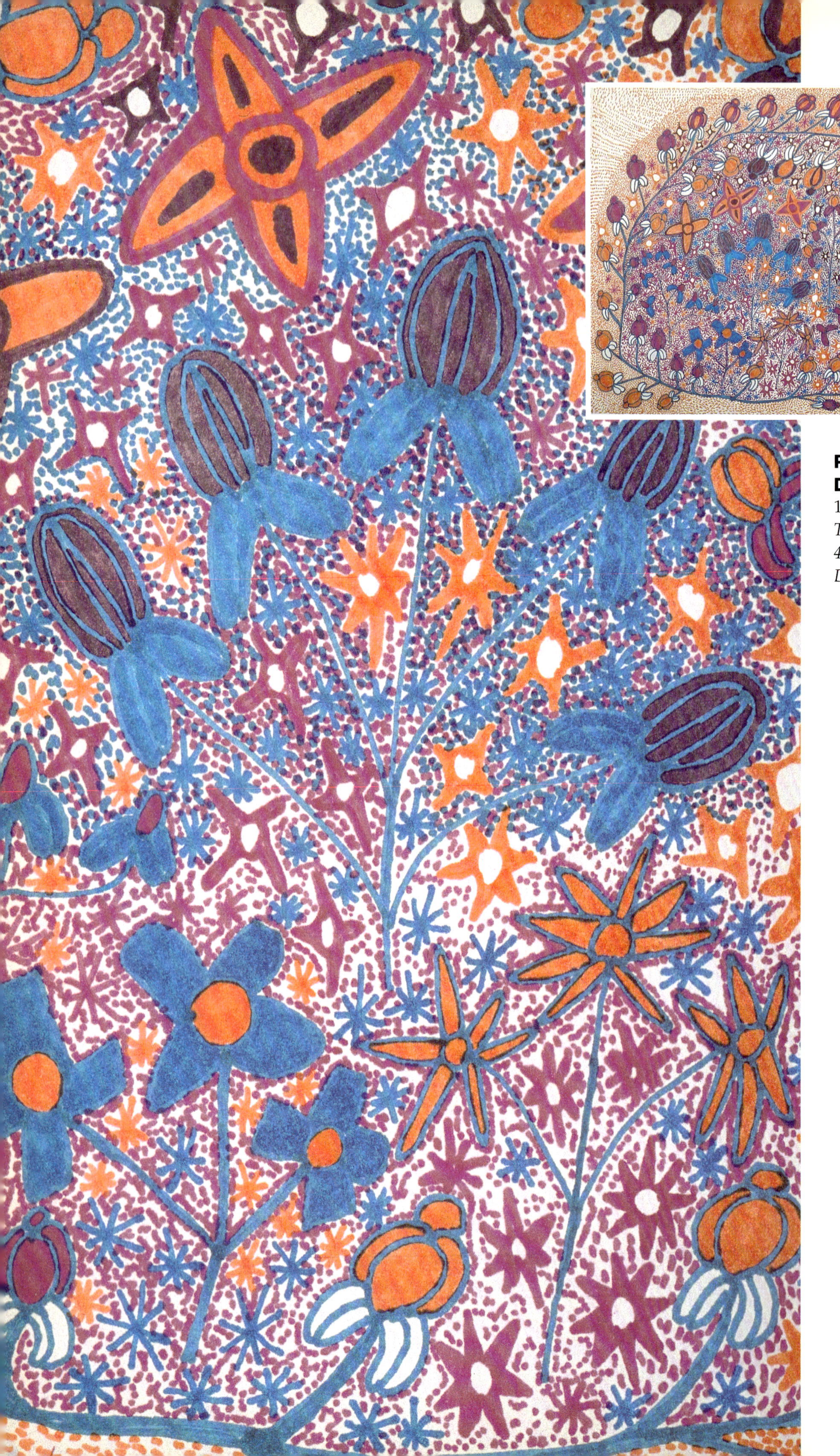

**Partiri –
Desert Wildflowers**
1986 / 89
Textacolour pen on paper
42.0 x 59.5 cm
Desert Designs Collection

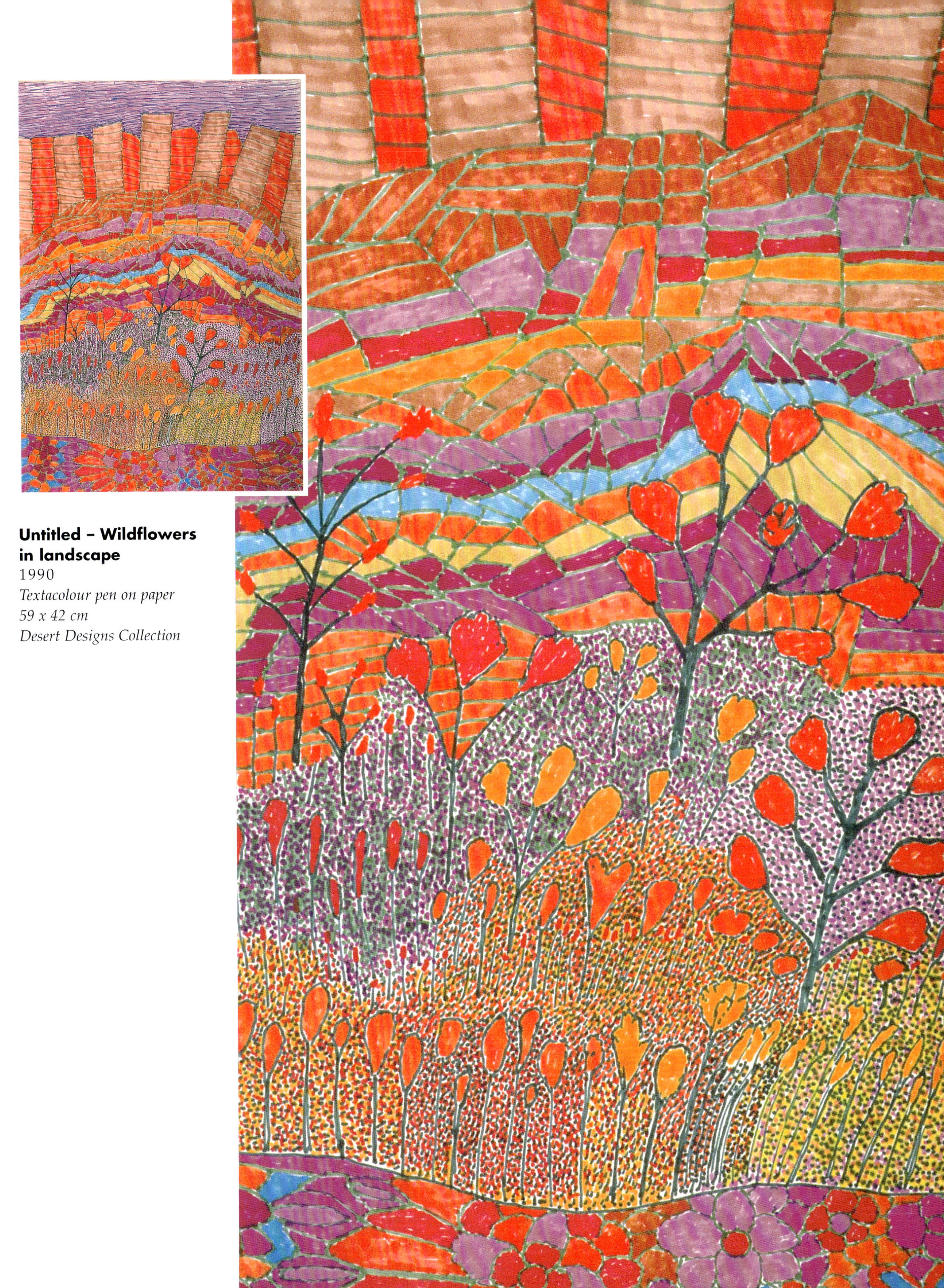

Untitled – Wildflowers in landscape
1990
Textacolour pen on paper
59 x 42 cm
Desert Designs Collection

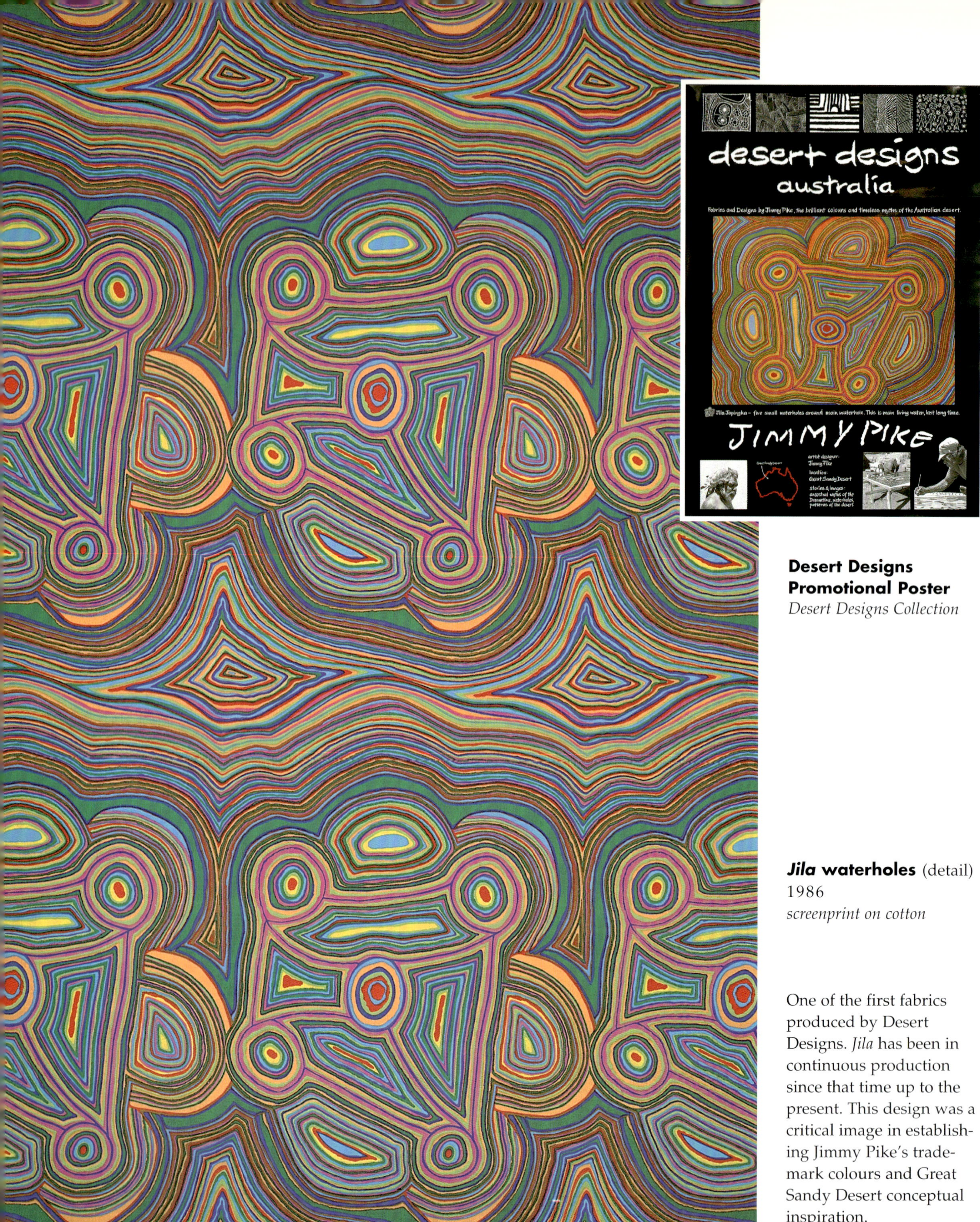

**Desert Designs
Promotional Poster**
Desert Designs Collection

Jila waterholes (detail)
1986
screenprint on cotton

One of the first fabrics
produced by Desert
Designs. *Jila* has been in
continuous production
since that time up to the
present. This design was a
critical image in establishing Jimmy Pike's trade-
mark colours and Great
Sandy Desert conceptual
inspiration.

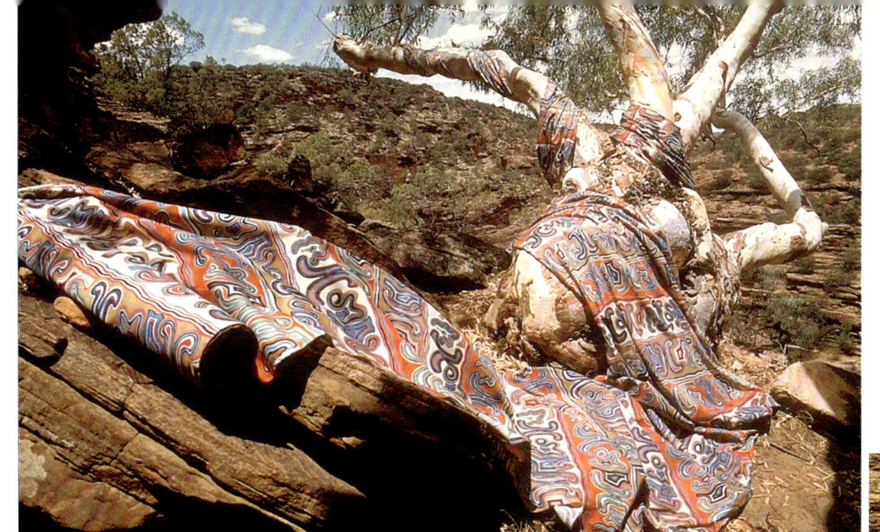

Dress fabric samples
1987
Byers Company, Sydney

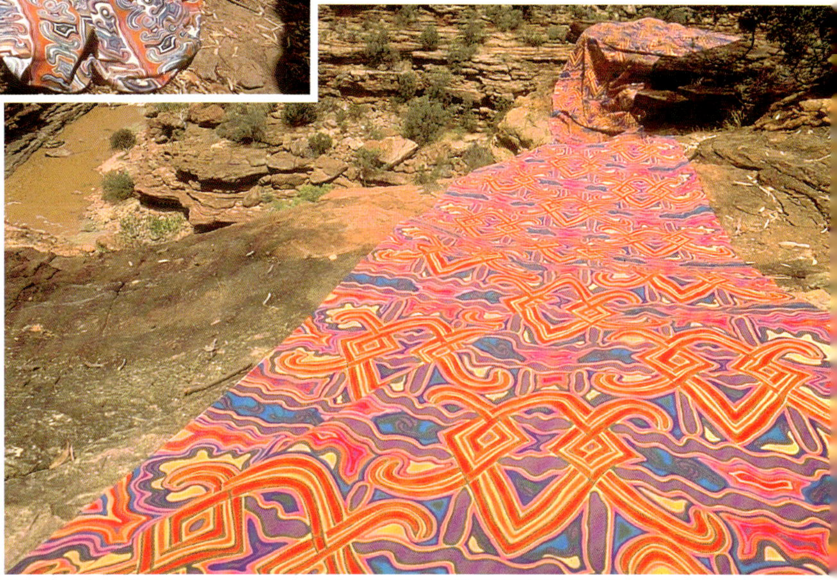

Bed linen 1986
Sheridan, Melbourne

National promotional image.
First total concept product line arranged
under licence by Desert Designs

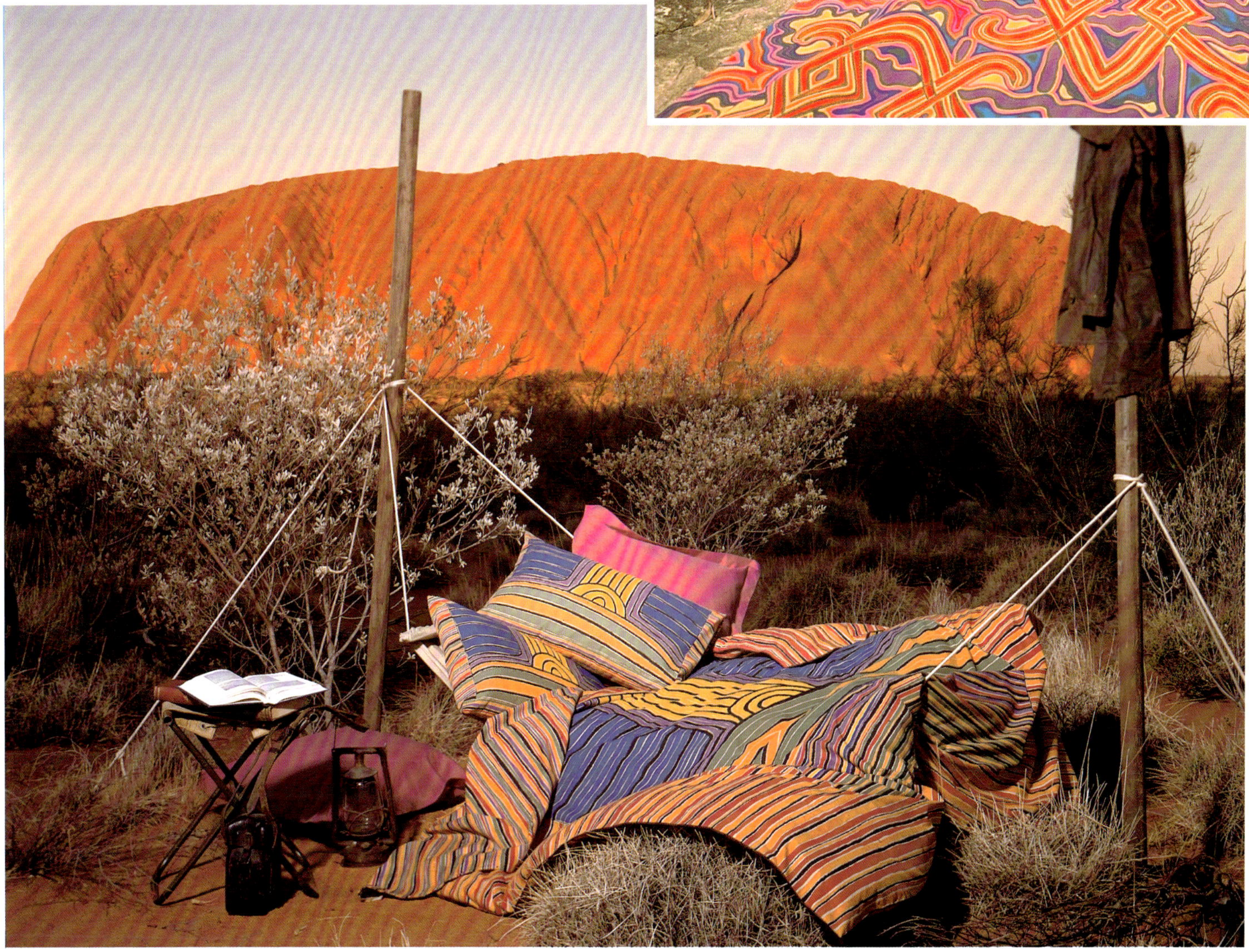

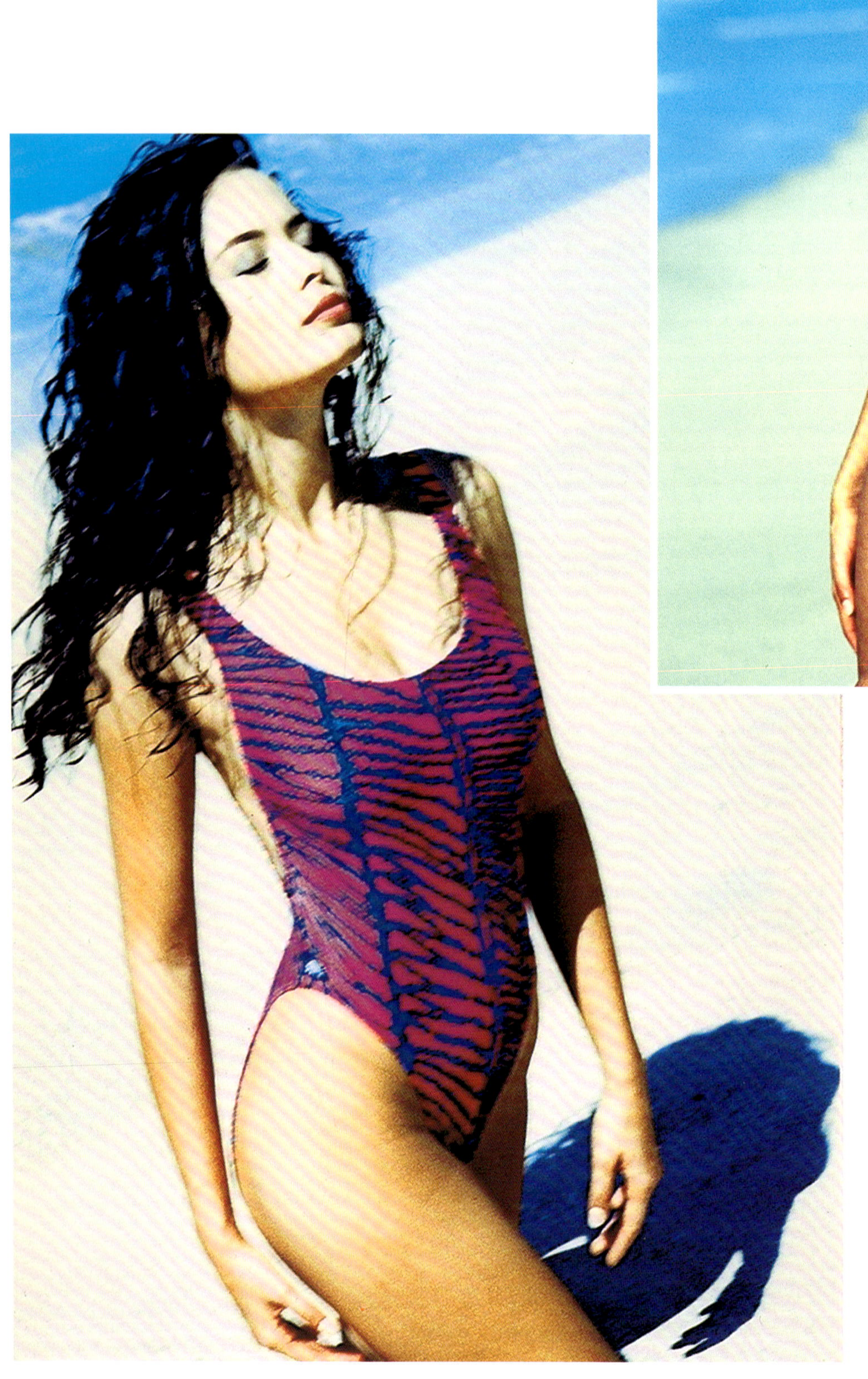

Swimwear range
1991
Moontide, New Zealand

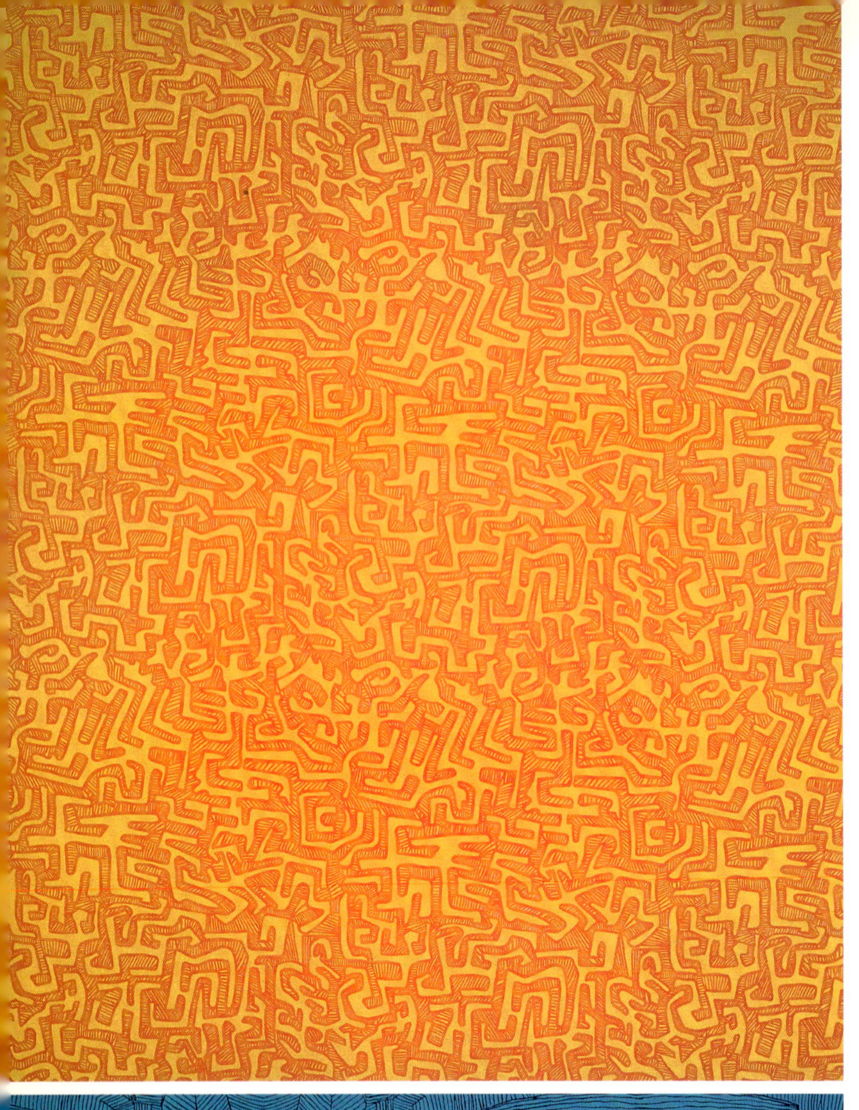

Jilji Kurmalyi
Sandhill design (detail)
1985
silkscreen on cotton
Desert Designs
manufacture

Early fabric production

Concept story board
1985
Desert Designs Collection

This is the first fashion design storyboard based around local Fremantle produced fabrics. Summer sports wear sold through local Perth boutiques. Lon Riley: designer.

Concept story board
1987
Desert Designs Collection

Summer fashion concept drawings. Produced as part of package for marketing new licensing promotion. Based around Byers fabric range.

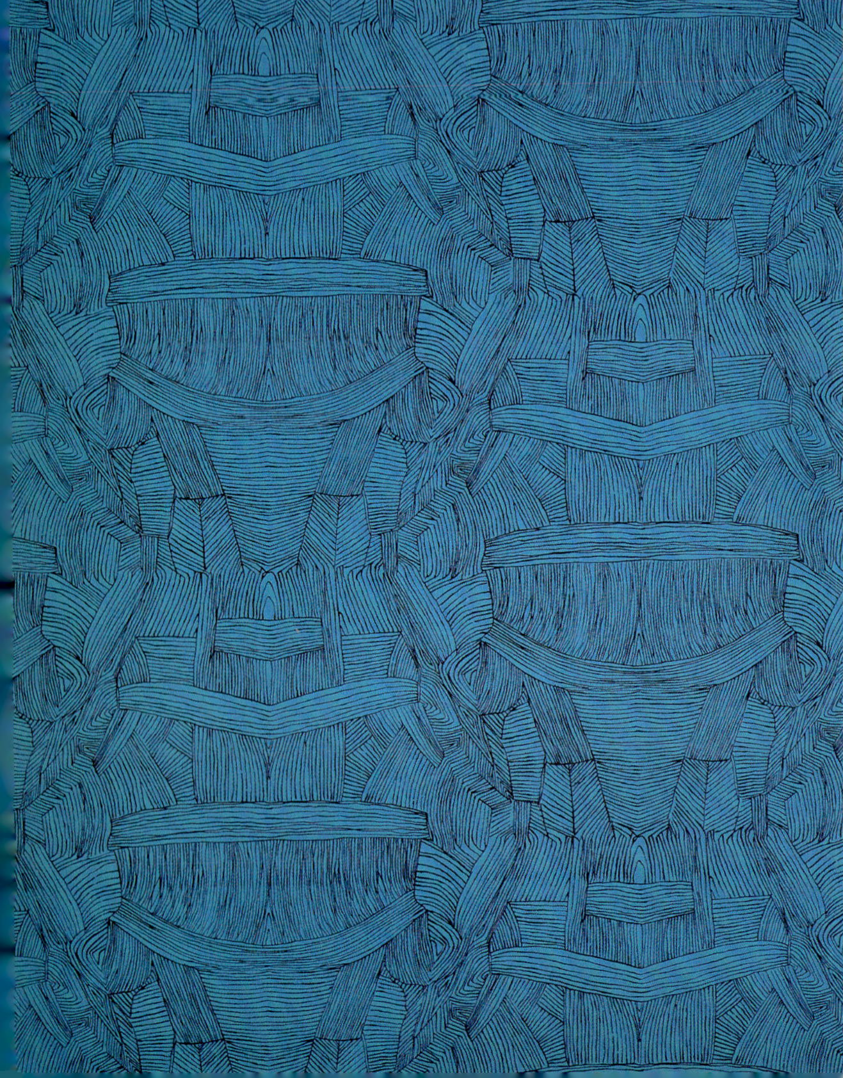

Jilji and Kurrkuminti
Maze design (detail)
1985
silkscreen on cotton
Desert Designs
manufacture

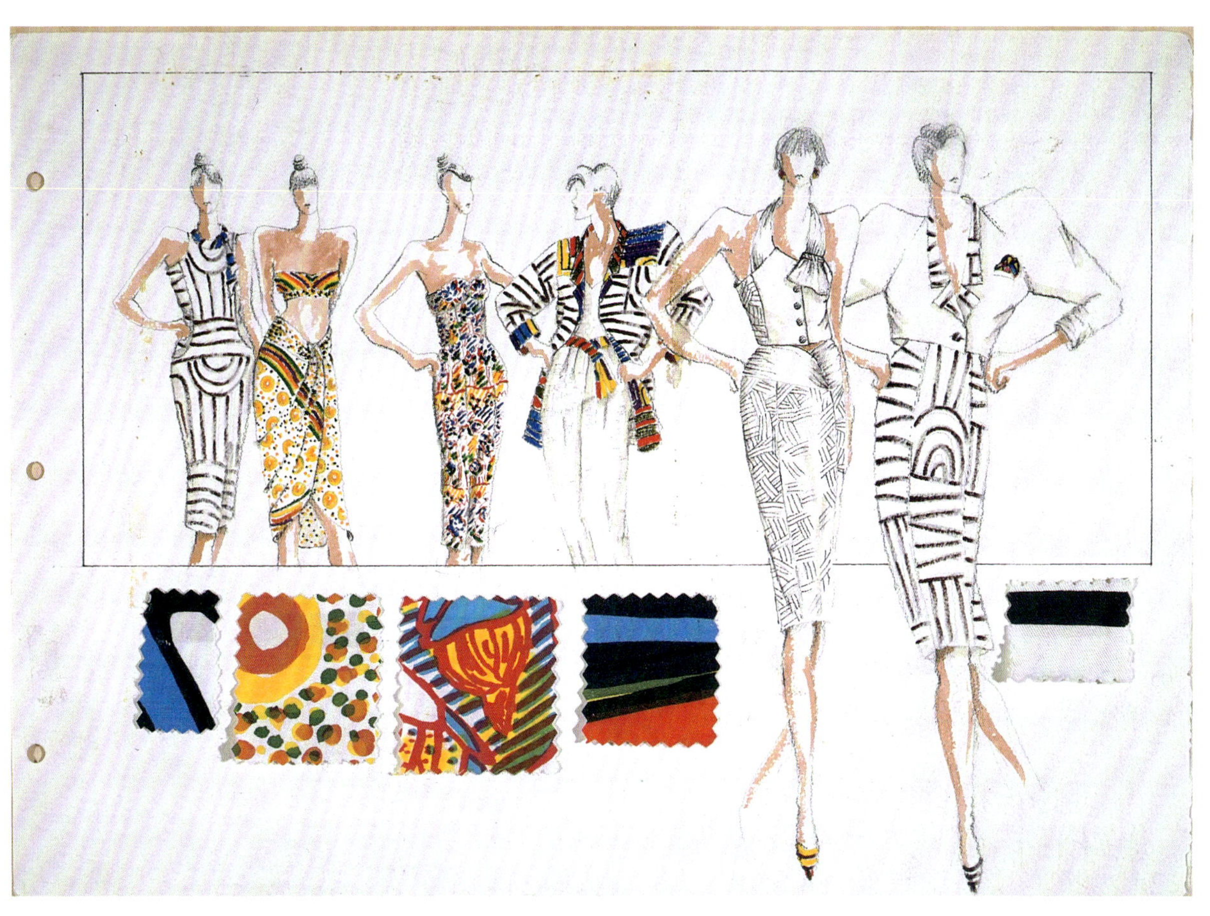

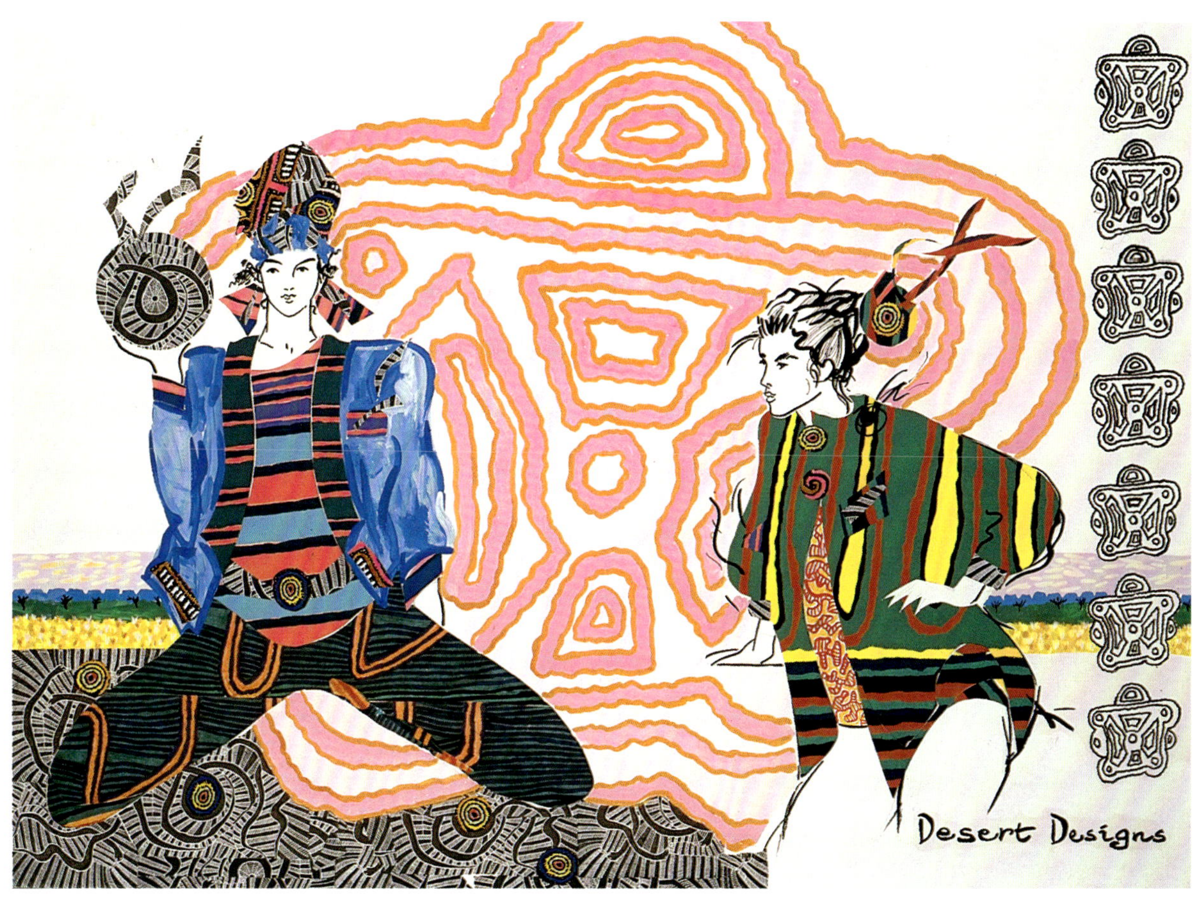

Desert Designs

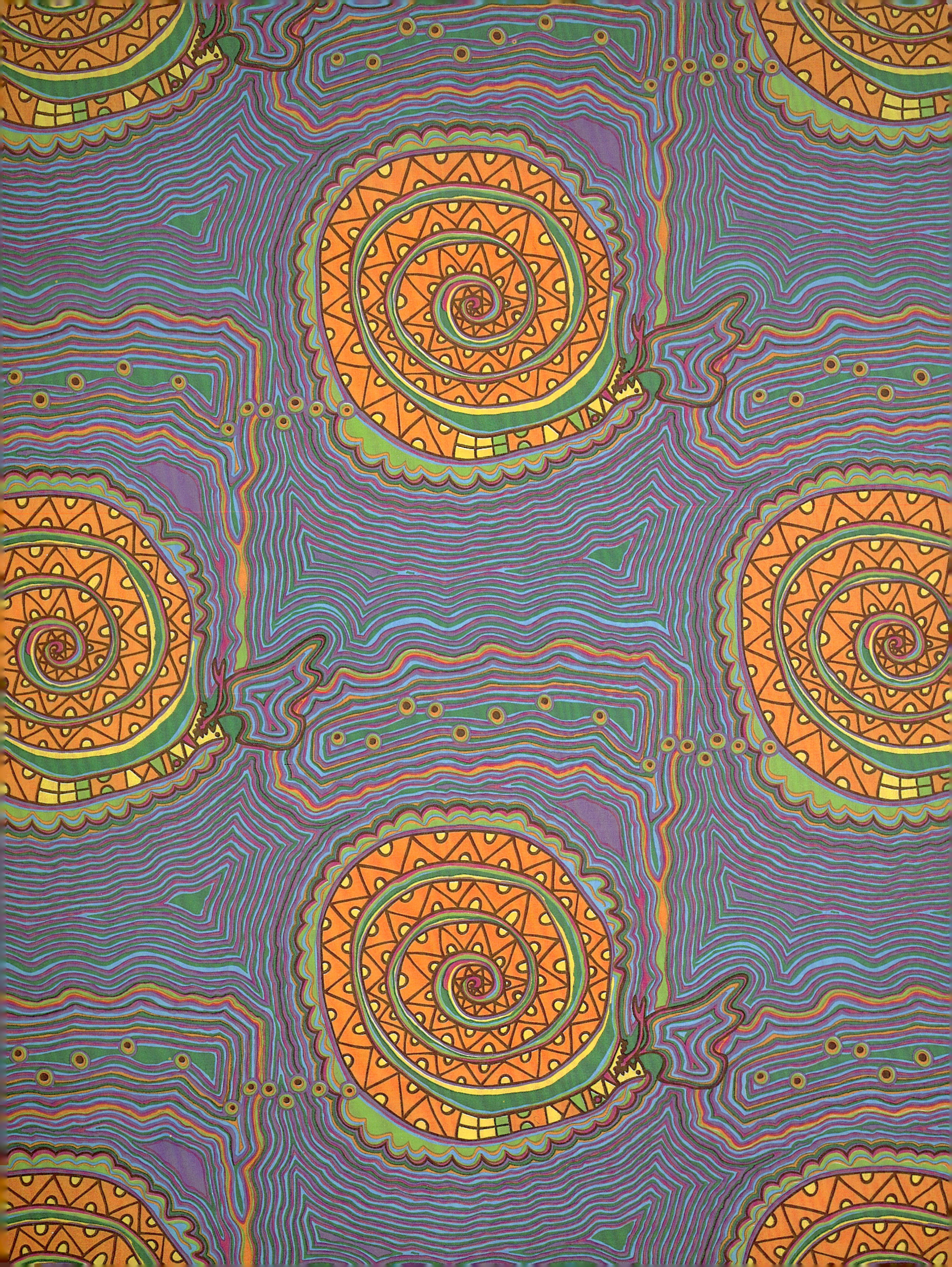

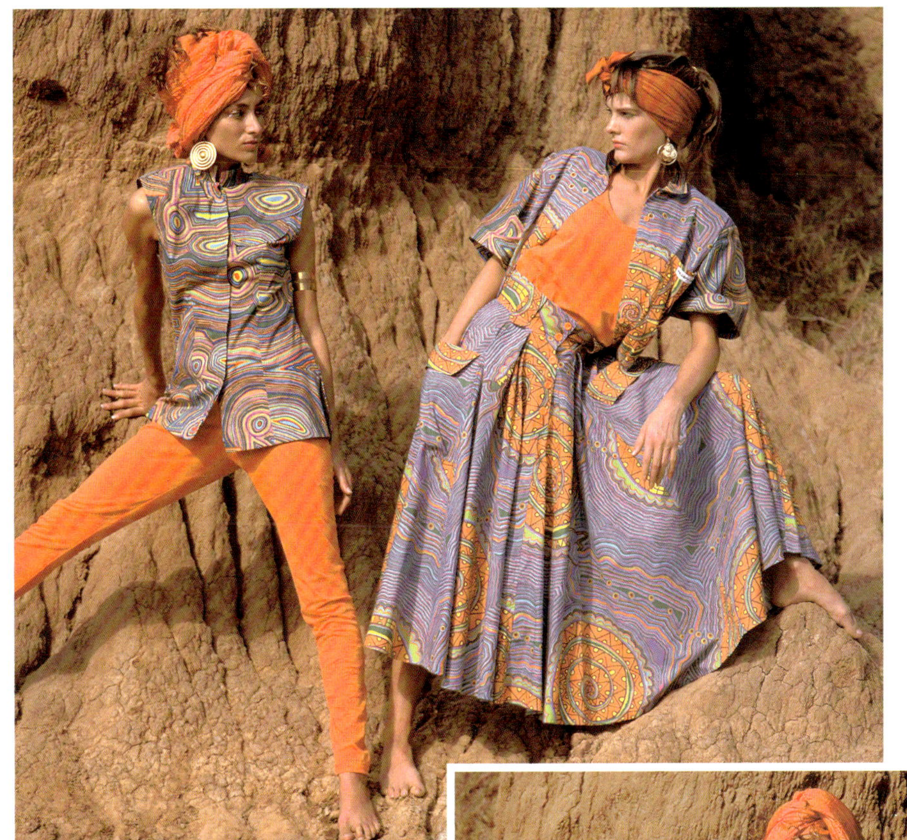

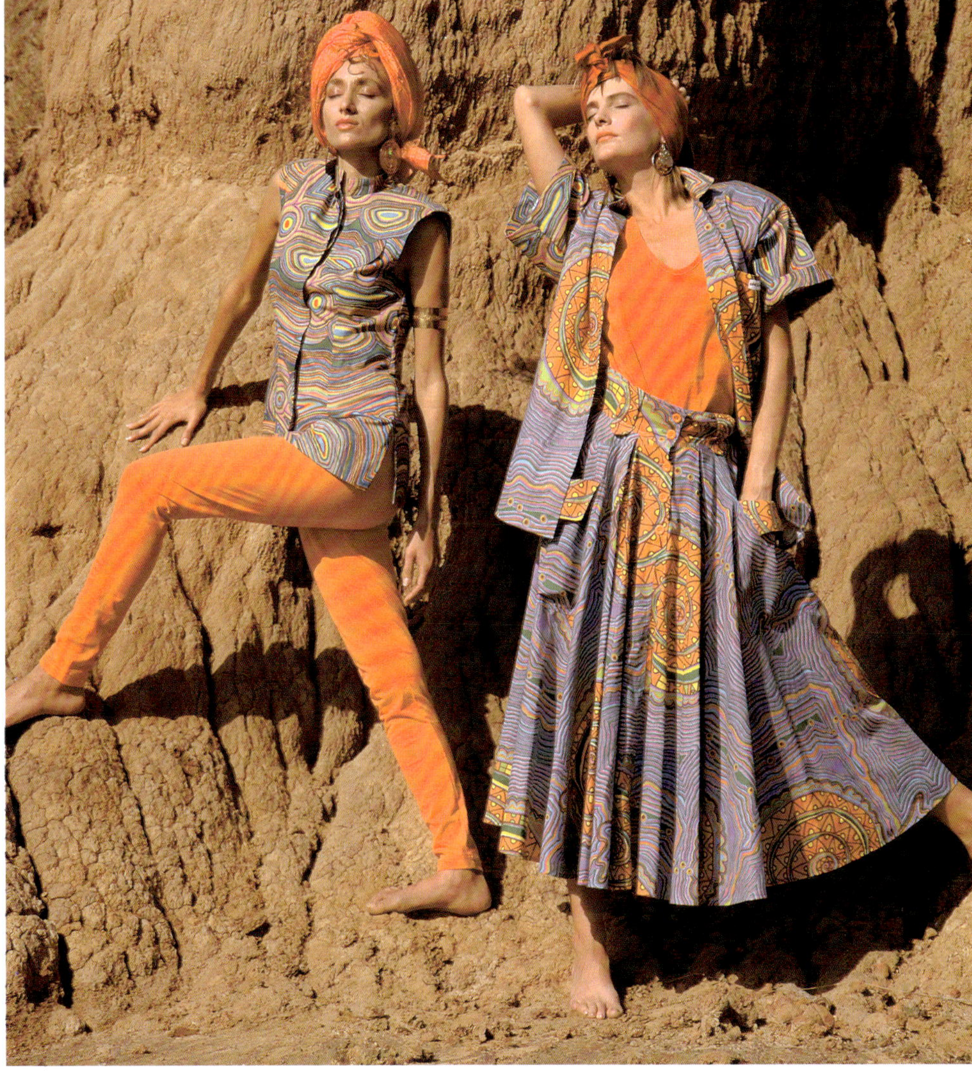

Kalpurtu
waterhole snake (detail)
1986
silkscreen on cotton

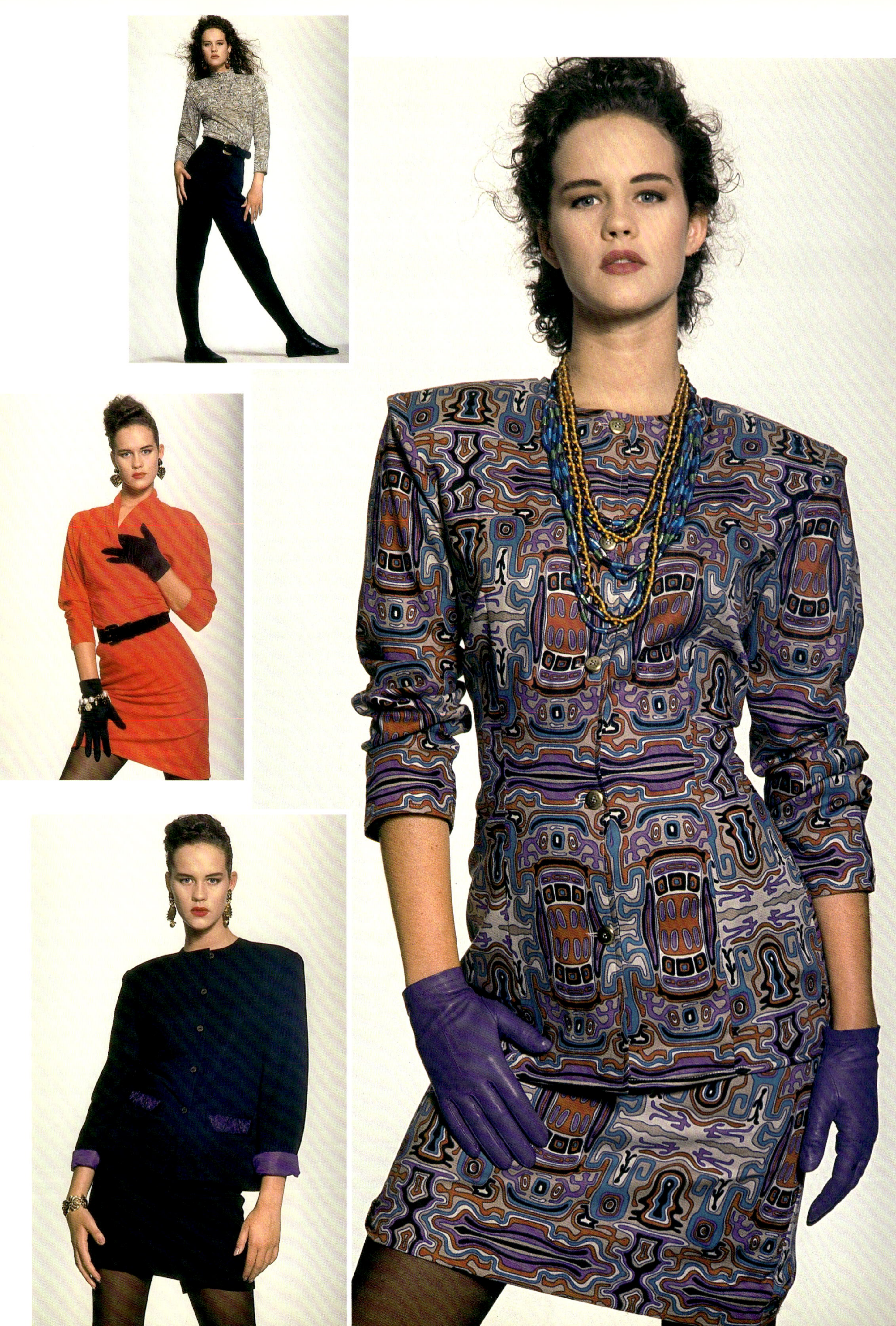

Men's wear 1989
Nevada shirts, Perth
Photographer: Leon Bird, Perth

Summer fashion range 1987
Byers Company, Sydney
Family group: adult and children's sports wear line.

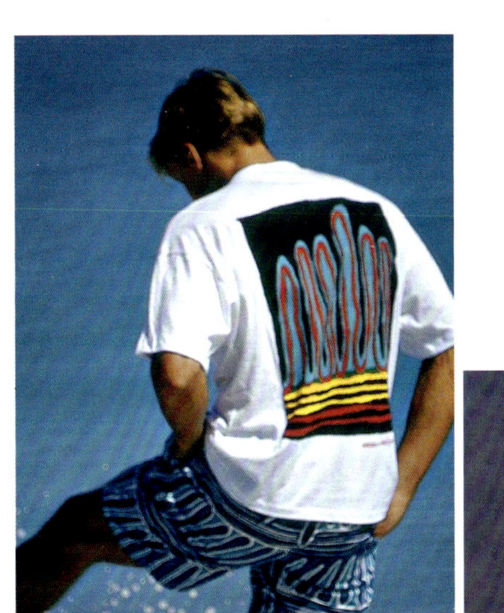

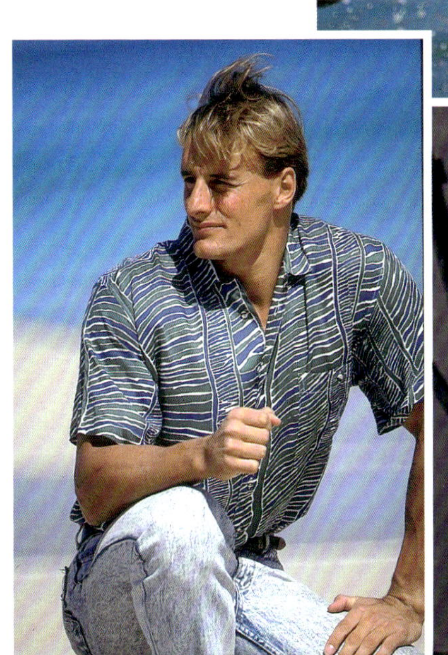

Winter fashion range
1987
Byers Company,Sydney

Beginning of full
seasonal collections.

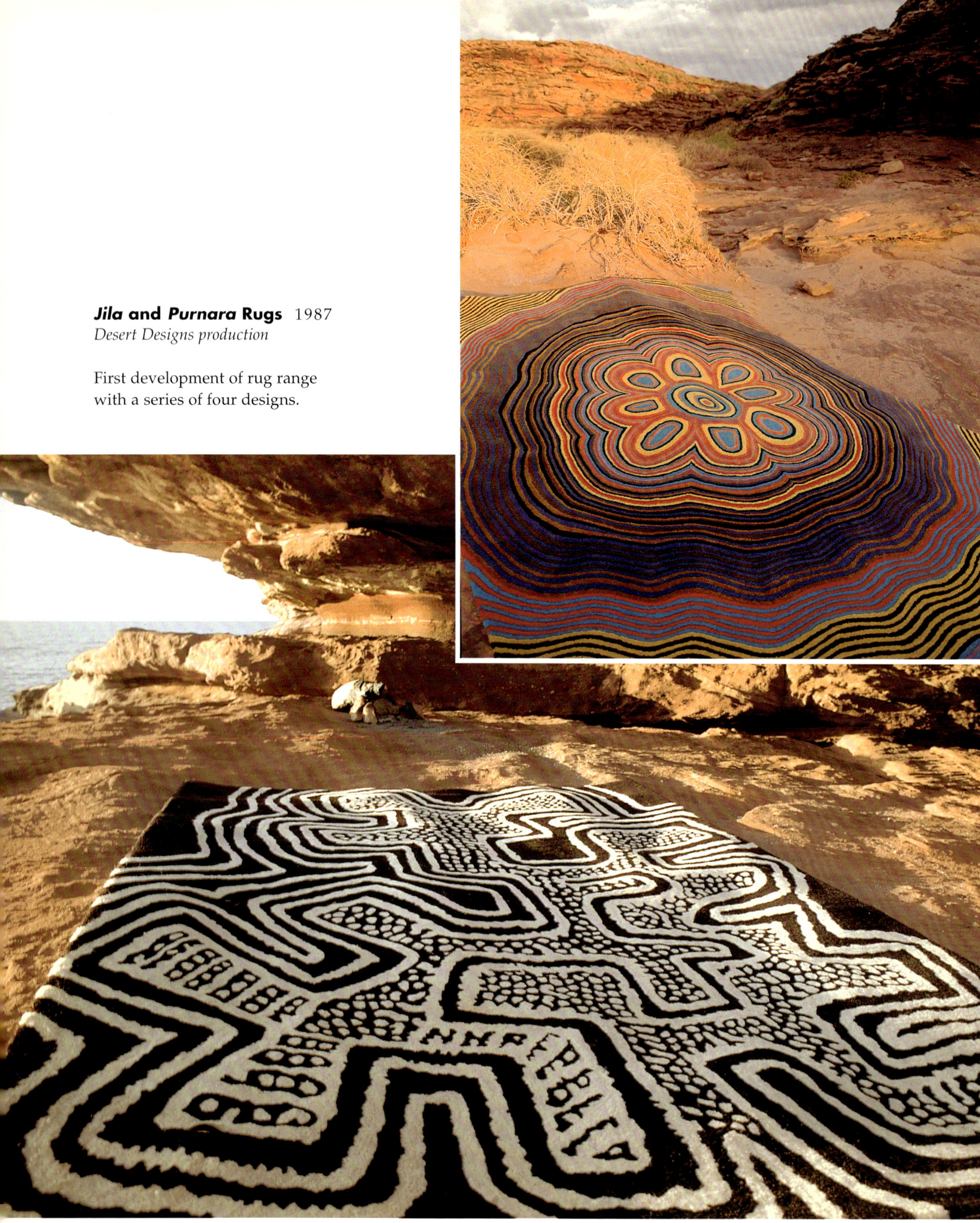

Jila and Purnara Rugs 1987
Desert Designs production

First development of rug range
with a series of four designs.

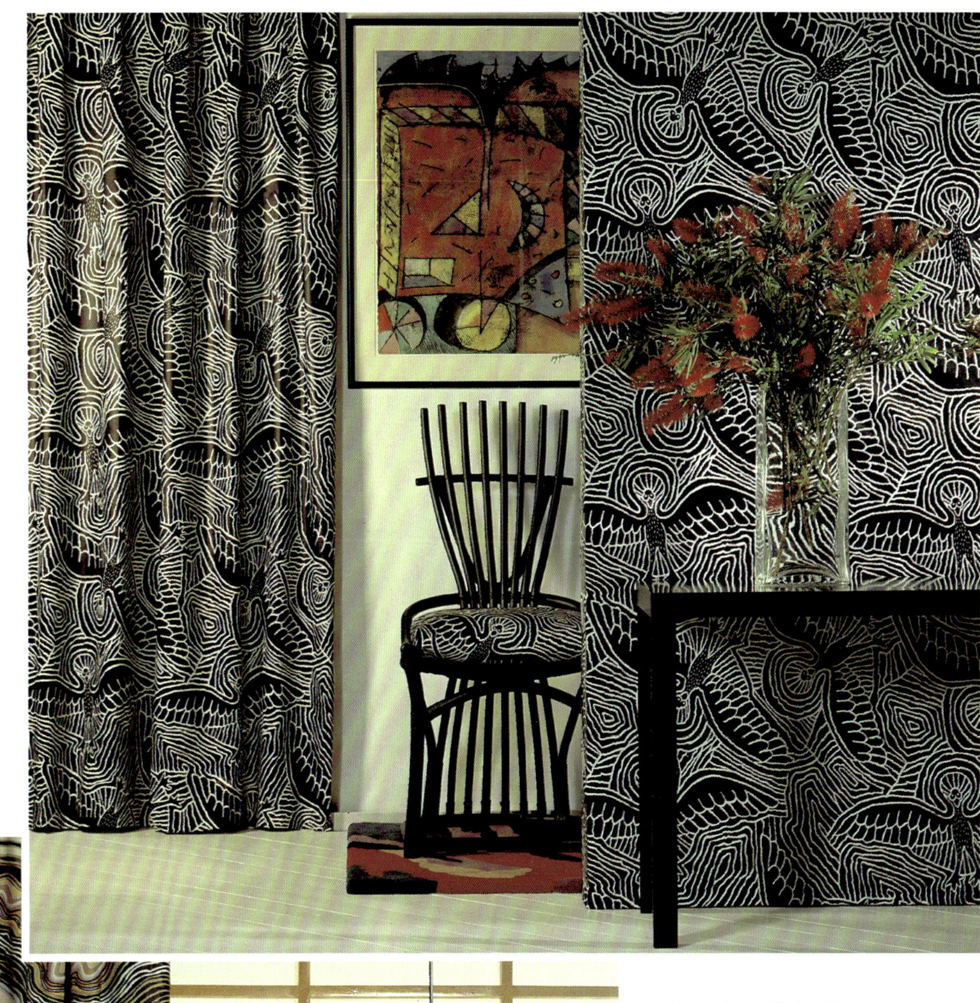

Interior fabrics
1989
Rowe fabrics, Sydney

First licensing arrangement
in home furnishings.

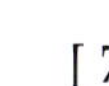

[75]

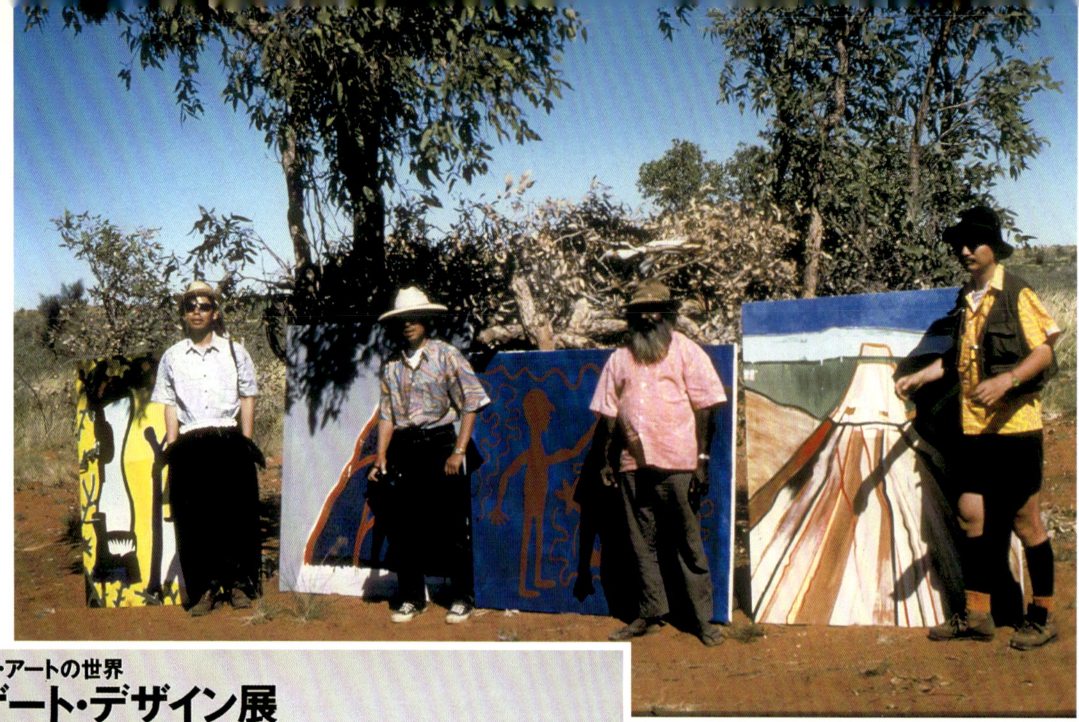

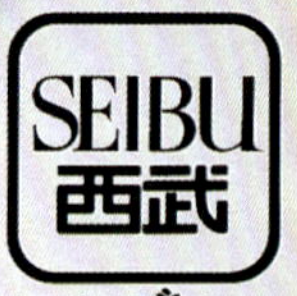

Kimberley artists' camp
1987

Artist Jimmy Pike and Japanese designers/artists in desert bush camp prior to August opening of Tokyo exhibition.

Exhibition Poster
Seibu Shibuyu, Tokyo
1987

This Seibu Departmental Store exhibition travelled to major cities on a six month tour after its opening in Tokyo. This was a total design concept exhibition featuring Jimmy Pike's prints, paintings and Desert Designs merchandising products.

Ski Wear   1990
Seibu (Asics Almos), Japan

First Desert Designs Japanese winter sports wear release.

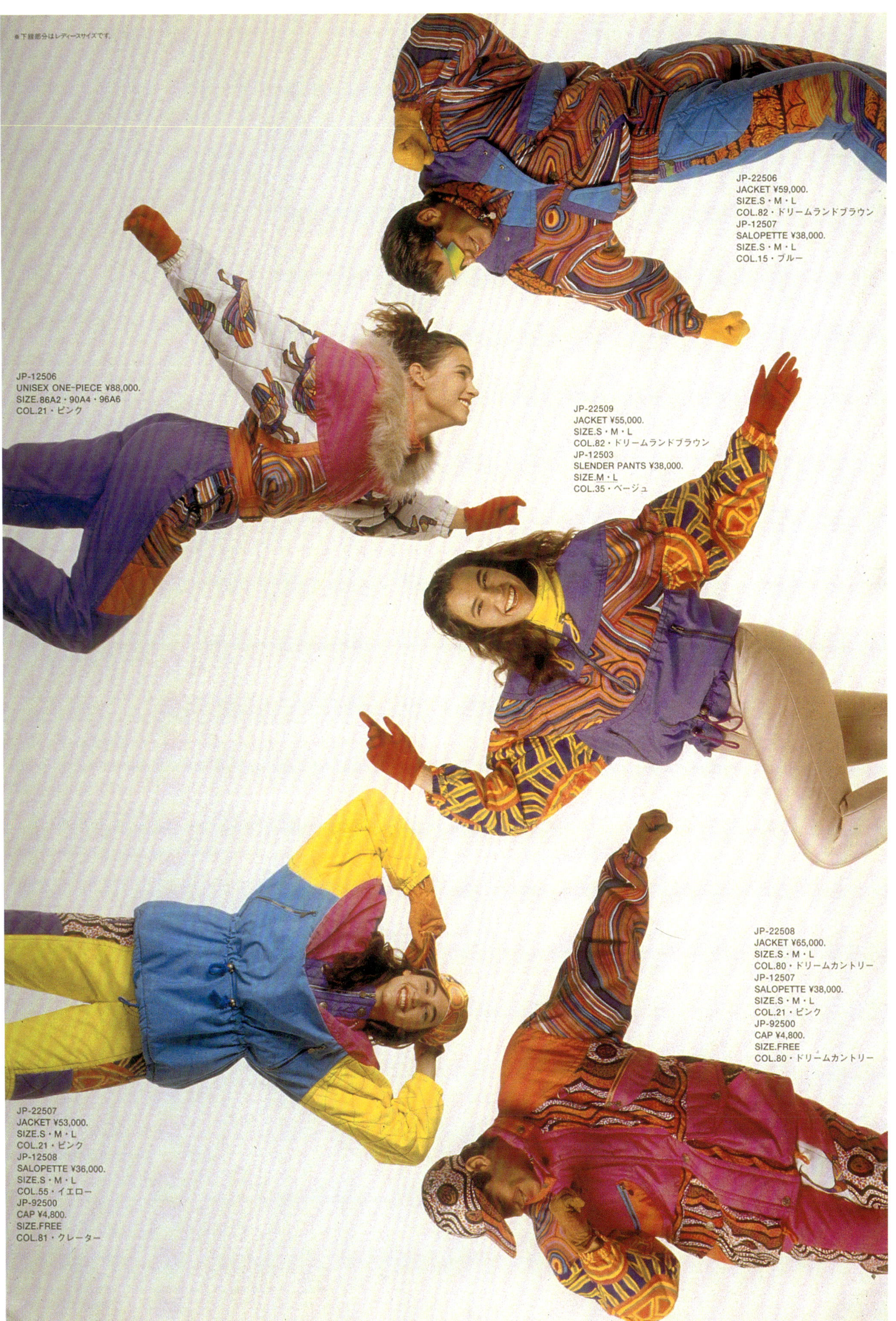

※下線部分はレディースサイズです。

JP-22506
JACKET ¥59,000.
SIZE.S・M・L
COL.82・ドリームランドブラウン
JP-12507
SALOPETTE ¥38,000.
SIZE.S・M・L
COL.15・ブルー

JP-12506
UNISEX ONE-PIECE ¥88,000.
SIZE.86A2・90A4・96A6
COL.21・ピンク

JP-22509
JACKET ¥55,000.
SIZE.S・M・L
COL.82・ドリームランドブラウン
JP-12503
SLENDER PANTS ¥38,000.
SIZE.M・L
COL.35・ベージュ

JP-22508
JACKET ¥65,000.
SIZE.S・M・L
COL.80・ドリームカントリー
JP-12507
SALOPETTE ¥38,000.
SIZE.S・M・L
COL.21・ピンク
JP-92500
CAP ¥4,800.
SIZE.FREE
COL.80・ドリームカントリー

JP-22507
JACKET ¥53,000.
SIZE.S・M・L
COL.21・ピンク
JP-12508
SALOPETTE ¥36,000.
SIZE.S・M・L
COL.55・イエロー
JP-92500
CAP ¥4,800.
SIZE.FREE
COL.81・クレーター

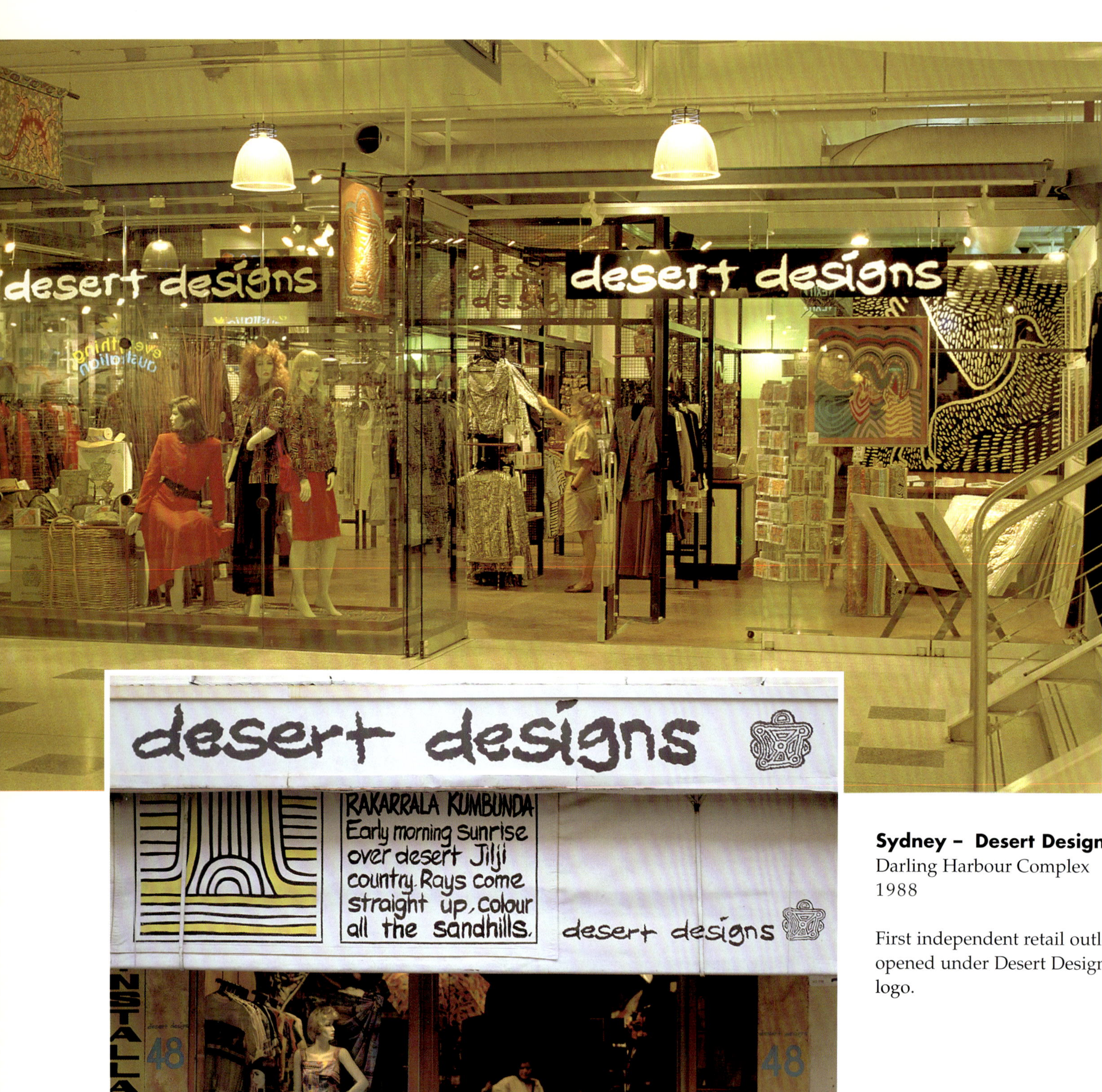

Sydney – Desert Designs
Darling Harbour Complex
1988

First independent retail outlet
opened under Desert Designs
logo.

Perth – Desert Designs
Fremantle 1988

First W.A store opened
in Fremantle.

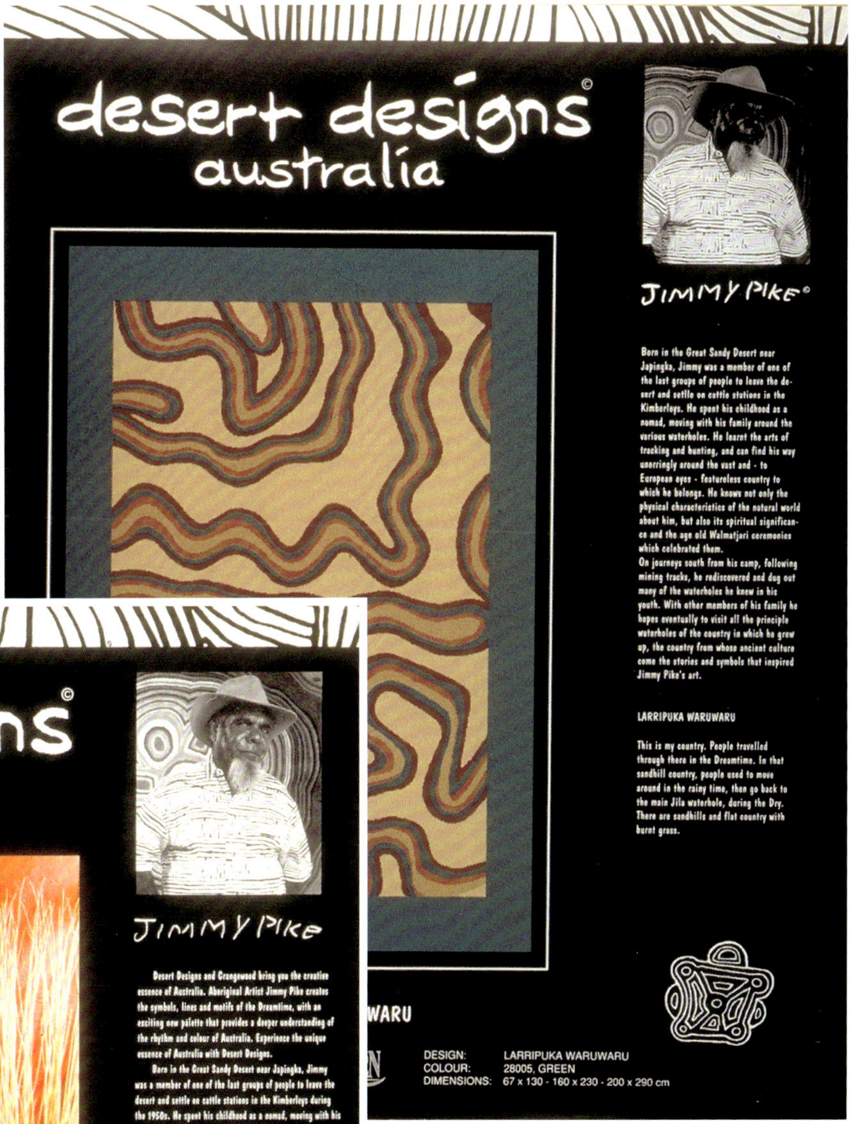

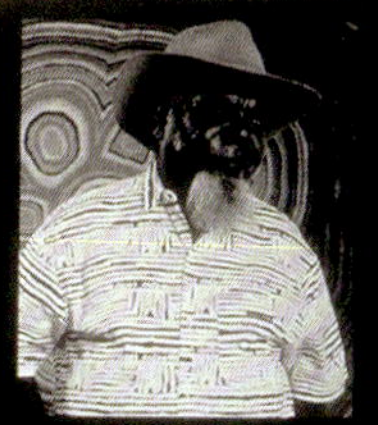

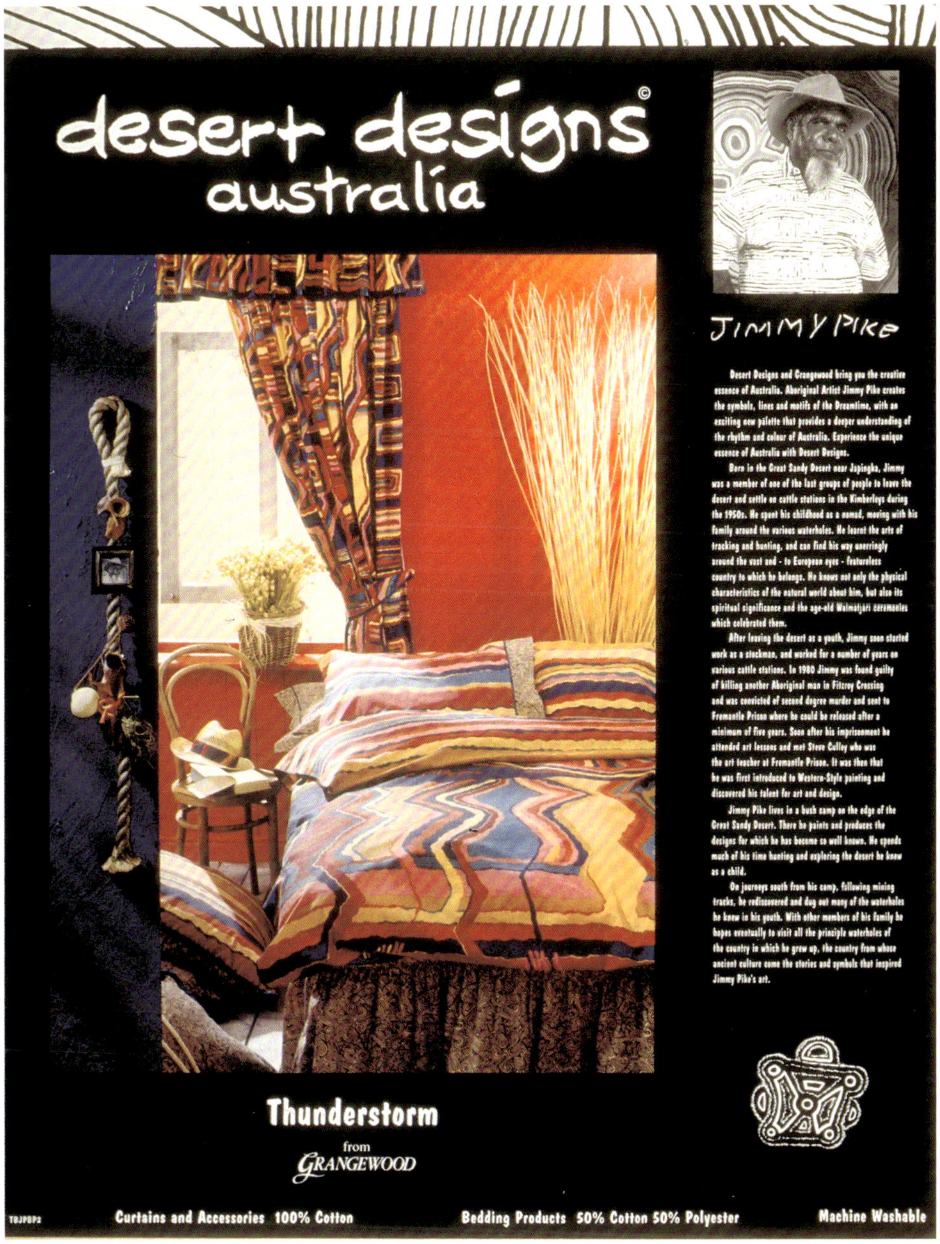

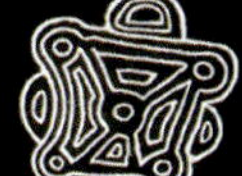

Interior/Home Furnishings
1992

First European Economic Community merchandise agreements.